Praying in the Spirit

What is it? Who can do it? How do we do it?

Terry Ivy

Praying in the Spirit

What is it? Who can do it? How do we do it?

Terry Ivy

Praying in the Spirit

What is it? Who can do it? How do we do it?

Published by 2T2 Publishing

Printed in the United States of America

For information visit: www.terryivy.com

Cover: 2T2 Publishing

Acknowledgement

A Special Thanks to...

Susanne, my lovely wife and best friend. You are a rock. Your constant encouragement and love fills my life with joy! Thanks for your tireless effort to finish this book. Above all, thanks for being my prayer partner, and for the many prayers you offer up for me. I love you more than words can express.

Yvonne, my Mom. I thank God for the example of prayer you have been. Only Heaven knows the amount of time you have spent before the Lord in prayer for others...and especially for me.

Carol, my sister in the Lord. Thanks for all your prayers for me over the years. Thanks for reading and praying through the manuscript and offering needed insights.

Dedication

To all those I have had the privilege to kneel
with in prayer and seek God's face.
Many are home now, waiting for me to join
them around the throne!

Table of Contents

Forward 17

Chapter 1 -

Laying the Groundwork 19

Chapter 2 -

The Foundation of All Things 25

Prayer with the Word

Chapter 3 -

Meditation 29

False Meditation

Biblical Meditation

Meditation—Our Quiet Time with God

Chapter 4 -

Desire, Discipline and Delight 43

Desire

Discipline

Delight

Chapter 5 -

All Prayer In The Spirit 51

The Holy Spirit's Work in Prayer

Chapter 6 -

Different Seasons of Prayer 61

Different Kinds of Prayer for Different Seasons

Summary

Conclusion

Chapter 7 -

Abba, Father 75

Humility

The Garden of Self Denial

Some Hindrances to Praying in the Spirit

Prayer is Work

Chapter 8 -

Paul's Rejected Prayer 87

Paul - A Man of Prayer

Paul's Thorn in the Flesh

Paul's Rejected Prayer

Paul's Submission to God's Will

Chapter 9 -

Praying in Tongues 95

Praying in Tongues is Praying "With the Spirit"

Praying in Tongues "in the Flesh" and "in the Spirit"

If a Christian has this Gift, How Much Should He Pray in Tongues?

The Purpose of Praying in Tongues

Am I Less Effective in Prayer if I do not have the Gift of Tongues?

Conclusion

Chapter 10 -

Ezekiel's Wheel 117

The Vision

The Application of Ezekiel's Wheel

The Momentum of Our Prayer

An Example of Praying in the Spirit

Conclusion

Chapter 11 -

Praying in the Strength of the Holy Spirit 129

What is Prayer?

Prayer is an Exercise of Faith

Prayer and the Will of God

Prayer Must be in Spirit and in Truth

Praying In and Through the Person of the Holy Spirit

Praying in the Strength of the Holy Spirit

Chapter 12 -

Answering Our Questions 141

What is Praying in the Spirit?

Who Can Do It?

How Do We Do It?

A Final Question

Chapter 13 -

A Final Word 149

Author Profile 151

Other Books by Terry Ivy 153

Forward

In prayer, God beckons us to understand his heart, and he enables us to know and obey his will through the Holy Spirit. We cannot properly follow Jesus unless we know where he is leading us, and the way we *know* is by learning to *pray in the Spirit.*

I have been fortunate to pray with many men and women over the years of my Christian life. These believers came from various theological backgrounds and experiences. This spectrum includes believers from Methodists to Baptists, from Charismatics to Presbyterians, from Pentecostals to Independents, from Wesleyans to Reformed. In each camp, I have come across those who were religiously dead, entrenched in tradition. However, I also became friends and prayer partners with many who were genuinely in love with Jesus and filled with the Spirit.

Most of these camps will explain *walking in the Spirit* a little different from the others. With that said, they will also define *praying in the Spirit* different from each other. However, I noticed that remarkably few, if any, ever discuss or offer a biblical explanation of praying in the Spirit. It seems that Paul's call for Christians to *pray in the Spirit* has been, for the most part, rarely explained or taught to believers.

For any work of God to have lasting effect, it must include prayer at its foundation. Those leading it must also depend on the Holy Spirit for their power. No believer, regardless of their level of education or theological background, should abandon the subjective work of the Holy Spirit—especially as it relates to prayer. We will look at several aspects to prayer; however, understanding the call and dynamics of *praying in the Spirit* is the thread which runs through every chapter.

You may not come to the same conclusions that I do, but one thing is for sure—we are called to be men and women of prayer. Any book we read on the subject of prayer that does not *compel us to pray* has failed. There is great need in our day for God to move on the hearts of men and nations, and it will only take place as the Church cries out to God in prayer.

The only success I desire to come from this book is for believers to enter into a life of prayer, and to discover the liberating and enabling power of God as we learn to *pray in the Spirit.* Prayer is the lifeblood of our soul.

Because of Calvary,

Terry Ivy

2017

Chapter 1

Laying the Groundwork

"Jesus Christ is the same yesterday and today and forever." (Heb. 13:8, ESV)

The purpose of this book is to help believers gain a clear understanding on the topic of "praying in the Spirit." This topic has been confused by certain circles who over emphasize the gift of tongues, or what they may call their private *prayer language.* I realize and am aware of the varying views concerning any discussion on this subject. I am also aware that many believers, who have the gift of tongues, believe that only those with this gift can *pray in the Spirit.* I believe this is a faulty interpretation and application of God's Word, and will attempt to clearly demonstrate that throughout this book.

If a person *idolizes*[1] the gifts of the Holy Spirit, what I write in this book may come across as a rejection of spiritual gifts for the modern church; be assured this is not my intention or position. I am only writing for the purpose of clearing up some of the confusion created by an incorrect opinion concerning the gift of tongues as it relates to prayer.

Also, if you hold to a position that all or some of the gifts ceased with the death of the Apostles or the completion of the writing of the New Testament, then you may disagree with some of what I share. I am sure some from both camps will disagree as sometimes it is difficult for believers to set aside their theological traditions and take a candid look at issues which others see differently. This book is not written in an adversarial or antagonist tone. Regardless of the position you hold concerning the gifts of the Holy Spirit that are mentioned in the New Testament, this book can benefit your understanding. We will look at many verses and issues for you to think about and work through.

My desire is very simple: to state clearly, from the biblical text, what is involved when Paul writes that believers should offer *"all prayer in the Spirit."* (Eph. 6:18) We will go wherever the Scriptures lead us. We will not dodge, for the sake of protecting a traditional position, any verse that challenges a denomination's teaching on this subject. Prayer is too important for us to trample under the feet of faulty

---

[1] By *idolizing*, I'm referring to the practice of some people who think that certain gifts of the Holy Spirit demonstrates their superiority over other believers, or that it means they are in right standing with God. It does neither.

interpretation or pet verses. In this book, we will seek to answer three questions:

1) What is praying in the Spirit?

2) Who can do it?

3) How do we do it?

Everyone reading this book has the right to know where I stand theologically on the issue of gifts. It is sad to me that we should even have to discuss or argue over things like this, but you have the right to know. While my position is not cessationism[2] concerning the gifts of the Holy Spirit, neither can it be classified as Pentecostal.[3] In other words, I believe

---

[2] Cessationism is the view that certain "gifts of the Holy Spirit" ceased from practice after the history of the early church. This position usually holds to a time of ceasing around the closing of the canon of Scripture late in the first century. It usually centers around Paul's statement in his epistle to the Corinthians. (1Cor. 13:8-12) There are various views and degrees of cessation within this area of theology. This position seems to build the case for rejection of some spiritual gifts on a very ambiguous passage, and it usually comes from those with a predisposition against supernatural manifestations. In the latest research, 50% of Southern Baptists pastors and 66% of non-SB pastors believe that the gift of tongues is still given to *some* believers today.

[3] Pentecostal belief holds that subsequent to salvation, every believer needs the "baptism of the Holy Spirit with the evidence of speaking in tongues." This causes believers to seek the gift of tongues. This doctrine is arrived at by neglecting sound biblical hermeneutics and focusing on select passages. Because of the emphasis on spiritual gifts and tongues, we see many *false gifts* within the church. We should let God decide who does and who does not get certain gifts. The purpose for all spiritual gifts is always the edification of the local church.

all the gifts of the Holy Spirit, whether you call them ministry, motivational, or charismatic gifts, are still present in the church and will be until the return of Christ. However, at the same time, I do not believe that *any one gift* is a sign of a deep work or a gift to every believer. We should always seek a mature understanding concerning the gifts of the Holy Spirit, and promote the edification of others while maintaining biblical order and decorum in our public meetings.

I have dear brothers on both sides of this issue. However, let me clearly state that while holding to the fact that Jesus is the same *"yesterday, today and forever"* (Heb. 13:8), including His right to distribute gifts as it pleases Him, I am also a strong supporter of holding to sound doctrine to prevent error, confusion, or excess. (1Cor. 14:39-40) Therefore, my position is that *all* the gifts of the Holy Spirit have been available down through the church age and will continue until Christ returns. Equally so, I believe much of what we see today, especially on religious television, are *false gifts*[4] masquerading as the work of the Holy Spirit.

In short, I do not fit into the 'either or' box some try to insist on. Why? Because I accept all the gifts of the Spirit, but I do not see tongues as a sign of the baptism of the Holy Spirit, or spiritual power—it is simply one of the gifts. *Every* believer is baptized into the Holy Spirit at salvation (1Cor. 12:13), and the gift of tongues is only given to *some* believers. (1Cor. 12:30) I am constantly finding that more and more

---

[4] *False gifts* are those which are manufactured by over-emotionalism, psychosomatic conditions, psychological pressure, or foreign spirits.

believers and leaders are moving to a balance from both sides of the issue concerning spiritual gifts, and this is encouraging. We should keep our focus upon Christ crucified and let God distribute the gifts as it pleases Him and fulfills His will. (1Cor. 12:11)

There is a great need for the *work* of the Holy Spirit in our day. Also, there is a great need for *sound teaching* about the person and work of the Holy Spirit. However, the greatest need is for us to understand prayer—for it alone is the source of our power to fulfill our call of ministry. Our work and accomplishment for God's kingdom is directly linked with our response to the call to prayer. And the success of our prayers is directly linked to *praying in the Spirit.*

This book is not about gifts, but about *prayer.* Therefore, we will not move into a deep discussion concerning gifts, though we must pass through some of the discussion about tongues because it relates to prayer. The claim by some that only those with the gift of tongues can pray in the Spirit requires us to do this.

Prayer is the lifeblood of the soul, and praying *in the Spirit* is the existential oneness between the believer and the person of Holy Spirit through prayer. It is of utmost importance that we understand what the Scriptures teach concerning it.

Within the pages of this book, we will focus upon and biblically define "praying in the Spirit." Hopefully we will clear up the misunderstandings and confusion about *what it is, who can do it* and *how do we do it.* I pray what we look at will open up rivers of truth concerning the work of the Holy Spirit in prayer. And that each of us would come to understand that in all things, especially prayer it is, *"Not by might, nor by power, but by my Spirit, saith the Lord of hosts."* (Zech. 4:6)

Prayer:

Father, teach us to get past the perception of religious labels and to look at the text of the Scriptures. Forgive us if we have used the exercise or rejection of the gifts of the Spirit for unscriptural divisions within your body. Mature us, Oh Lord. In Your name, Amen.

Chapter 2

The Foundation of All Things

"We have also a more sure word of prophecy; whereunto you do well that ye take heed..." (2Pet. 1:19)

"Beloved, believe not every spirit, but try (test) the spirits whether they are from God:" (1Jn. 4:1)

The Bible must be the basis and final authority of every activity in the believer's life. God has given the Church the roadmap for navigating through the various minefields of doctrine, life, and experience. In other words, we must allow the truth of the Scriptures to have the final authority to determine the accuracy and legitimacy of any spiritual claim. We must *not* interpret the Word through our experiences. Instead, we *must* allow the Word to interpret and judge our experiences. There are many people having spiritual experiences and calling them encounters with God.

However, upon biblical examination we discover that many of these experiences are either artificially contrived, self-prompted by emotional needs, brought on through psychological pressure from a false minister, or demonic. We must learn the difference.

In short, the Lord has given us the Word as a safety net to protect us from foreign or counterfeit experiences. We do not have to be afraid of becoming deceived by supernatural experiences as long as we judge and discern each one *before* we accept them as authentic. Every intimate encounter with the Lord is a spiritual experience, and most of them will take place in the quiet time of prayer and meditation.

Prayer with the Word

During prayer times, both corporate and private, we are reaching out for guidance, comfort, encouragement, or insight from the Lord. The Holy Spirit is the person of the Godhead who moves upon our heart, spirit, and mind to show us God's direction and insight. Jesus promised that the Holy Spirit would be the comforter to *guide us* into all truth. (Jn 16:13) Any genuine communion with the Lord is always accomplished through the ministry of the Holy Spirit.

Prayer is the most direct and intimate encounter we have with God on a continual basis. Because of this, we are constantly receiving impressions and promptings in our spirit from the Lord. We need to be careful that the promptings we receive are from the Holy Spirit and not from foreign sources. This is why the Scriptures play such a vital role in the life of every believer; it provides us with an objective standard whereby to test and examine every subjective experience.

If we are concerned about whether a teaching is from God, run to the Scriptures. If we wonder about whether an impression is from God, run to the Scriptures. If we are concerned about whether an experience we have in prayer is from God, run to the Scriptures. As long as we are men and women of the Word, we will be protected from religious foolishness and false spiritual claims or impressions.

We have a sure foundation and it is trustworthy! Let us cling to the sound teaching of the Scriptures, and while we do, let us refuse to be afraid of receiving authentic spiritual encounters from the Holy Spirit. The Lord wants to pour himself into and through our lives as we spend time with him in prayer.

Today, we see enough dry religious meetings to last a lifetime. We need a fresh outpouring and encounter with God. Also, there are enough false spiritual experiences taking place to last a lifetime. We need genuine encounters with the Holy Spirit, and we will recognize them because they will pass the truth test of the Scriptures.

One of the reasons praying *in the Spirit* is so beneficial to our walk with Christ is that it delivers us from dry religious formalities and breathes spiritual life into our prayers. Likewise, because we hold the Scriptures as the ultimate authority, we need not recoil from the spiritual experiences we may have while praying in the Spirit. God's Word protects us from embracing the religious foolishness created through false impressions.

We all should seek to know and pray the will of God. Understanding how to do this is the goal of this book on prayer. The Lord wants us to be like children concerning malice, but like adults concerning understanding. (1Cor. 14:20) The more we understand the multiple layers of application in the discipline of prayer, the more successful and equipped we will be as men and women of prayer. Knowledge brings authority and power, and this is certainly true concerning prayer.

However, all the knowledge in the world is useless if we never step out in faith and put to work what we know. Let us guard against learning apart from application. Knowledge alone will only *"puff us up"* in pride if we fail to act upon what we know. (1Cor. 8:1) Therefore, let us take our knowledge about prayer, along with the authority of the Scriptures and the love of God as our impetus—and pray!

Prayer:

Father, settle in us the conviction of the absolute truth of Your Word so that we can be free from fear and trepidation toward the supernatural work of Your Spirit. Take us out of our strength and into Your strength so we can accomplish Your work on the earth. In Jesus name, we pray, Amen!

Chapter 3

Meditation

"I will meditate also of all thy work, and talk of thy doings." (Psa. 77:12)

"I will meditate in thy precepts..." (Psa. 119:15)

"Meditate upon these things; give thyself wholly to them..." (1Tim. 4:15)

Meditation is a term which is seldom heard among Christian communities today. In fact, we read and hear many warnings against Christian meditation. And yet, we see throughout the Scriptures the call to meditate upon the truths of God, especially in the Psalms. We also see Paul calling us to be renewed in our mind in several of his epistles. (Rom. 12:2; Phil. 4:8) However, we meet few believers who understand or have been taught about the method, purpose, or benefits of biblical meditation.

Western culture usually views the practice of meditation with a suspicious eye, thinking that only people in Eastern cults or mystical religions practice meditation. We must guard against throwing the "baby out with the bath water." Just because the world perverts a practice or discipline of faith does not mean we should abandon it. We need to reclaim every truth from God which has been robbed from the church by false religions.

Meditation is an *essential* part of praying in the Spirit. However, we must always be careful not to get swooned into the counterfeit practice of it. In this chapter, we will discuss the difference between the practice of false meditation and biblical meditation. We will see there are *clear distinctions* which separate the real from the false.

FALSE MEDITATION

In order to prevent us from becoming fearful of participating in the practice of unbiblical meditation, let's begin looking at some of the distinguishing factors which will help us identify it. First, let's define the secular or eastern definition of the word meditation. Pay careful attention to the words in bold.

> *"Meditation is related to 'mediation,' as between two parties, to bring together insight and behavior. Emphasizing meditation* ***without content*** *cultivates total openness for receiving the cosmic vision of the ideal order of things.* ***Contentless meditation****, in which the mediator*

transcends entirely, is generally identified with Zen Buddhism. It cultivates limitless receptivity, or an ***emptying of the mind****, as it is described. Even where a Koan (mediative paradox) is used as a focal point, as in Zen,* ***its function is to wear out the reason and grasping mind and so to empty it. "No mind" is the goal.****"*[5]

Notice how the entire purpose of this type of meditation is for our minds to become *passive* and *empty*. This passivity is pursued in order to get the mind to suspend discernment and for the individual to receive every spiritual impression placed upon him. As we will see in the next section of this chapter, this is *contrary* to the practice of Christian meditation.

An empty mind is open for *something else* to fill it. A passive mind is not alert to judge what that something else is. This is the basis for strong demonic activity. Demons pray on empty and passive minds in order to fill them with deceitful suggestions and impressions. Their influence is greatly enhanced by passivity because this gives them the green light to work their schemes without the concern of being uncovered.

Some of this masquerades in Christian circles as the work of the Holy Spirit. I have heard many ministers teach false meditation principles to unsuspecting believers without realizing they are encountering demons instead of the Holy Spirit. Many present day teachings on prayer are no more

---

[5] Encyclopedia Americana

than the practice of yoga and other Eastern religions mixed with Christian teaching. False meditation includes several different practices.

Yoga

Yoga is a technique used in many Eastern and Hindu philosophies. The aim of yoga is a mystical connection and unity with the Supreme Absolute Being by giving up all worldly ties, by eradicating all desire and passion. One may begin by concentrating on a red flower or a blue circle: from these early stages one proceeds to develop the power of meditation until one attains the trance of union with the infinite. This final state is called "Samadhi," and it involves the fading out of the mind.[6]

Yoga in False Christianity

Yoga, of course, is contradictory to Scriptures because its goal is to *fade out the mind.* In Christianity, believers are called to have an active and alert mind. Again, many practice and teach the concepts of yoga under the guise of Christian doctrine. Any teaching that calls for man to cease from reason and to become passive is straight from the teachings of yoga and is not Christian.

When men seek experiences for the sake of experiences, rather than seeking encounters with the risen Christ, they become guinea pigs on the altar of secular or religious mysticism. There are many experiences which are available

---

6 *"Religions of the World Made Simple"*

for those seeking them through yoga. This is important: the experiences within the practice of yoga, transcendental meditation, repetitive prayer, and non-Christian meditation are real. However, *they are not truthful.*

Channeling and Astral Projection

New age gurus and their channeling[7] experiences are real spiritual encounters, but they are demonic in origin. Many movie stars, business executives, and even your neighbors are having wild and bizarre experiences through the techniques of false meditation. We will never reach them as long as we brush off these experiences as "not real." They are real; they are just not truthful or biblical.

A few years ago I had an in-depth conversation with a man about meditation. He claimed to be a Christian, and at the time, seemed to have a passion for Christ. In our discussion, he began describing how he was experiencing out-of-body travels while meditating. (Astral projection) This man attempted to use one of Paul's experiences as a proof text for the legitimacy of his experience. As he continued to discuss his out-of-body travels, it became clear that he sought them by seeking passivity through unbiblical meditation. His experiences were real but they were not from God.

I was able to take him through Paul's explanation of his spiritual experience and show him the difference between

---

[7] *Channeling* is the practice of becoming passive and being taken over and controlled by a spiritual entity.

the real and the false. (2Cor. 12:2-4) He listened intently, but rejected my warnings and admonitions of how he was playing around with demonic activity. Sad to say, I saw him years later, and his life was one of destruction, loneliness, and confusion. Satan had dangled the carrot of false meditation in front of him and produced spiritual death in his life. This is why it is so crucial to know the difference between the false and the biblical forms of meditation.[8]

Passivity

We can sum up the major theme of false meditation with one word: *passivity*. Passivity is when the mind becomes concentrated on one thing to the point of losing reason to anything else. It is also when the mind becomes blank, and the will is surrendered to anything—from voice or movement or impression. Passivity is a fundamental law for the working of demonic spirits through humans. If Satan can persuade us to become passive, then he knows we will fail to judge the impressions he sends to us and that he can lead us into blind obedience.

The Scriptures never command or teach us to become passive. In fact, we are taught just the opposite. We are to use our mind, reason, and *all of our faculties* as we commune with the Lord. The Lord tells us to come *"reason together"* with him. (Isa. 1:18) He requires submissive, but active co-operation, while demons seek and desire a passive person.

---

[8] Please see my book, *"Trying the Spirits"* to learn how to use the principles of Christian discernment.

Biblical Meditation

Let's now turn our attention upon the characteristics of *true* biblical meditation. We are called to wait upon the Lord. This waiting is a vital part of praying in the Spirit because this is when we die to carnal impulses in order to wait for the Lord's direction. This is where biblical meditation comes into play for the believer.

In biblical meditation, we are called to maintain a *proper state of mind.* Let's look at several different mindsets which believers can have.

Unrenewed Mind

This is a mind which has not been renewed in its thinking because the person is a young believer—a babe in Christ. (Rom. 12:2) Our mind is renewed as we spend time studying the Word of God and allowing the Lord to refashion and reestablish the foundation for our thought patterns and the governing principles of truth. We learn how to think properly (Phil. 4:8), to think out of *agapē* love (1Cor. 13:4-7), and to think from Christ's perspective. (Phil. 2:5) In short, as God's children, we are given the *"mind of Christ."* (1Cor. 2:16) The more we are established in the truths of God's Word, the less likely we will be tricked by Satan's impressions. An unrenewed mind will yield to every whim or imagination the world offers as truth, even if separated from any form of reality.

Anti-Warfare Mind

This is a mind that receives any and all suggestions and thoughts presented to it. We will frequently find this in believers who fail to understand or acknowledge the war that believers face against the powers of darkness. (2Cor. 10:4-5; Eph. 6:17; 1Pet. 1:13) We are called to resist the devil, not ignore him. (Jas. 4:7; 1Pet. 5:8-9) We must faithfully embrace our call and responsibility to stand against the schemes of the enemy. (Eph. 6:11) Just because a statement or opinion is proclaimed to be true does not make it so.

Passive Mind

As we saw in the previous section, this is a mind that becomes concentrated on any one thing to the point where all reasoning is suspended or shut down. It involves blind obedience to any voice or impression. This includes a blank mind. A passive mind is an *incredibly dangerous state* for believers to have. This can happen if we desire something so strong that we focus upon it with extreme intensity and abandon discernment. A passive mind causes us to become *open for any impression*. If the impression makes us feel good, we will think it must be God's will. We will fail to recognize the spiritual trap the enemy is setting for us because a passive mind has suspended judgment.

Transformed Mind

This is the mind that has and is experiencing a daily renewing from God's Word. This mind is active and in a warfare state. (Rom. 12:1-2) A transformed mind tests all things by means of spiritual reasoning. (1Cor. 2:13-15) God calls us to *understand* his will. (Eph. 5:17) This requires an active and pursing mind on our part.

Biblical meditation is always performed with an *active mind* and from a pure heart. Let's take a look at some of the Scriptures which show us how our mind is to be active throughout our Christian walk, including the times of prayer and meditation. The words beside the references are from these verses and show activity, and not passivity.

* Philippians 4:7-8, "understanding, think"
* Isaiah 26:3, "whose mind is stayed upon thee"
* Psalms 5:1, "meditation"
* Matthew 22:37, "all thy mind"
* Romans 8:5-6, "spiritually minded"
* 1Corinthians 2:12-13, "know, comparing"
* 1Corinthians 2:16, "mind of Christ"
* Philippians 3:16, "let us mind the same thing"
* Colossians 1:21, "enemies of your mind"
* Colossians 3:1-3, "set your mind"
* Colossians 3:12, "humbleness of mind"
* 2Timothy 1:7, "sound mind"

*Hebrews 8:10, "my laws into their mind"

*1Chronicles 16:15, "be ye mindful always"

Jesus teaches us to love God with *"all our heart, mind, soul and strength."* (Mark 12:30) This involves the totality of what man is—all his faculties, talents, and gifts. The Lord is the one who gave us our mind, not to abandon or neglect, but to use. At salvation, the Holy Spirit begins washing our thoughts from the influence of a humanistic worldview. Then he begins reestablishing the foundation of our reasonings with the truth of God's Word. He replaces the wisdom of the world with the wisdom of God. We have a paradigm shift from self-centeredness to Christ-centeredness, and from moral relativism to an absolute moral truth.

The Lord re-trains us to think as children of light. This training makes us wise and discerning, not passive and vulnerable. It also gives us confidence to call out in prayer for all the Lord has for us because it provides a foundation to test all things. That foundation is the truth of Scriptures.

Paul instructs believers to *"meditate upon"* the things he gave as instructions. (1Tim. 4:15) This compound word in the Greek (*meletaō*) means to "take care of; revolve around in the mind." The practice of biblical meditation involves an *active pondering* and reflection upon God's Word and his promises. We may be in a quiet place and saying nothing verbally, but our mind is pondering upon the things of God. During these times of reflective thought and pondering in prayer, we are engaged in the practice of biblical mediation.

Meditation—Our Quiet Time with God

Biblical meditation is our quiet time with God. This does not mean we must always be alone in a quiet place to meditate on the Lord and His Word. We can find the quietness of the Holy Spirit's presence in the midst of the bustle of our day. However, we should seek times of solitude in quiet places to pray and seek the mind of the Lord as a regular practice. This is how meditation becomes such a *vital* part of *praying in the Spirit*. The Lord trains us to pursue his personal direction through waiting, patience, and prayer. He slows us down and protects us from making knee-jerk reactions and impulsive decisions.

The proper state of biblical meditation is a pure heart and a spiritual mind. When we keep our sins confessed up to date, we maintain a pure heart. When we pursue God's truth and wisdom, we maintain a spiritual mind. From a pure heart and spiritual mind, we can have confidence about the Holy Spirit's leading because we seek no agenda or purpose other than to do God's will. God created us to understand his purposes and plans for our life. When we maintain a pure heart and walk spiritually minded, our soul seeks to know and remain faithful to God's will—not ours.

Biblical meditation is a state of the heart which involves *quietness of our soul*. Quietness does not mean passivity, where the mind is dormant and without reasoning. Instead, this quietness is *inner stillness* that is free from anxiety and the driving desires of the flesh. Our mind is alert, but refrained from actions in other directions, including healthy ones, in order to pray and pursue understanding from God. In this quietness, the mind is awake to every function in our environment, but it is directed toward communion with the Lord.

It is a healthy practice for believers to have a regular time of quiet meditation in a *place of quietness.* Once we begin enjoying this time of quietness on a daily basis, it will become a delightful discipline in our life. We will refuse to forfeit it because of the enormous benefit it becomes to our walk with Christ.

King David, in the first Psalm, describes meditation and the benefits of it.

> *"Blessed is the man that walketh not in the counsel of the ungodly, nor standeth in the way of sinners, nor sitteth in the seat of the scornful. But his delight is in the law of the LORD; and in his law doth he* ***meditate day and night****. And he shall be like a tree planted by the rivers of water, that bringeth forth his fruit in his season; his leaf also shall not wither; and whatsoever he doeth shall prosper." (Psa. 1:1-3)*

In this passage, David mentions seven benefits of biblical meditation.

*Not walking in the counsel of the ungodly.

*Not standing in the way of sinners.

*Not sitting in the seat of the scornful.

*We will be like a tree planted by the rivers of water, having deep roots in the love of God. We will always enjoying a fresh flow of the Holy Spirit.

*We will bear fruit in our season.

*Our leaves and their fruit will not fade in the heated trials of life.

*Everything we do, because we are submitted to the will of God, will prosper.

These are powerful promises to us if we spend time meditating on God's Word. Like Gideon's fleece (Judges 6:36-38), let us lay ourselves purely and quietly before the Lord in prayer, and allow him to pour the dew of heaven upon our life. When we do, we will begin buckling up the *"loins of our mind"* with godly reasoning, and we will discover the refreshing that comes from *thinking* on the proper things in life. (1Pet. 1:13; Phil. 4:8)

So much awaits us if we begin spending quality time with the Lord in prayer and mediation. As we have seen in this chapter, understanding and practicing biblical meditation is a necessary part of *praying in the Spirit.* The reason is because meditation is the aspect of prayer where we give ourselves to quiet reflection in order to discern the will of God for our life. Once we understand the Father's will, the Holy Spirit empowers us to offer it in prayer. And because it is the Father's will, we will have confidence that our prayers are heard and that the Lord will grant our petition.

Prayer:

Father, teach us the benefits of meditation, so that our time with you does not become a monologue from us. Reveal to us how in the quietness of our spirit You lead us by Your Spirit. Amen!

Chapter 4

Desire, Discipline and Delight

"I delight to do thy will, O my God:" (Psa. 40:8)

Prayer is the lifeblood of our soul. It is the source of our spiritual nourishment and communion with the risen Lamb of God. Satan hates it and will fight tooth and toenail to keep us from developing a mature prayer life. After all, it is through prayer that the truths of Christianity become embedded principles within our heart, producing a change in our disposition and clear direction for our Christian walk.

The Holy Spirit is *always* calling us to prayer. His promptings are rooted in our need for spiritual maturity and growth. Jesus gave us the Holy Spirit to teach us, guide us, fill us, convict us, enable us, empower us, and gift us. We must not neglect the work of this heavenly host.

After we become a new creature in Christ, our heart begins to cry out to the Lord in prayer. We feel the Holy Spirit pulling upon our soul and calling us to more time in prayer and into *deeper* prayer. As we respond to the Spirit's plea, we usually experience three stages of development in this path of prayer: desire, discipline and delight.

Desire

In the heart of every born-again believer is the *desire* to have intimate fellowship with the Lord. This desire is as natural to a genuine believer as an infant's desire for his mother's milk. It does not have to be conjured up, taught, or coerced—it is part of the new birth.

If a man does not *desire* fellowship with Christ through prayer, he is lacking genuine salvation and only has a religious profession. If a man has the desire to spend time with the Lord in prayer, but struggles with doing it, he either has unconfessed sin in his life or lacks understanding about the dynamics of praying in the Spirit. Yielding to the Holy Spirit's ministry in prayer is one of the greatest opportunities and privileges of our life in Christ. As we learn to yield to the 'tug of the Holy Spirit,' he will remove the struggles and obstacles hindering us from praying.

Let's look at two reasons why believers struggle with prayer.

Unconfessed Sin

If we harbor *known* sin in our heart, we will struggle with engaging in quality prayer. Sin hinders the intimate fellowship between the Lord and a believer. We should be thankful that it does because it is one of the ways the Lord confronts our sin and compels us to face it. When a believer realizes the loss of fellowship with the Lord he desires to repent and restore intimacy. For the genuine Christian, intimacy with the Lord is more important than the pleasures of sin!

When we harbor known and unconfessed sin in our heart, it is amazing how the Holy Spirit makes that sin *the issue* of our life. It becomes the Holy Spirit's focus as we approach the Lord in prayer. We may attempt to offer prayers concerning other things, but the Holy Spirit will continue to remind us of our sin and our need to repent.

Even when a true believer is struggling with sin, he will still have an inward desire to commune with the Lord through prayer. It is as certain as a fish seeking water—it is our environment. However, until we confess our sin and come clean with the Lord, we will struggle to have a life of prayer because of sin. It is hard to talk to the Lord about other things when he insists on continually discussing our need to repent.

Lack of Understanding

If we keep our sins confessed up to date, but lack the understanding about the dynamics of praying in the Spirit, prayer will become a drudgery or wearisome event in our Christian life. We may press through from time to time in remaining faithful to pray, but we will lack the liberating passion and joy to continue doing it. Desire *alone* will not make us successful in prayer.

When we learn that the *empowerment to pray* is the job of the Holy Spirit, we are released from the dreadful obligation of attempting to maintain a commitment to pray by our efforts alone. The Lord wants to teach us how to pray *in the Spirit* and free us from turning prayer into a self-serving and self-empowered fleshly commitment. This is why learning the dynamics of praying in the Spirit is so vital to a healthy prayer life. The Holy Spirit desires to enable and empower us in prayer. He becomes the wind *beneath* our prayer wings.

DISCIPLINE

Once we surrender to the drawing of the Holy Spirit for us to seek intimate communication with the Lord in prayer, we go through what I call the *discipline* stage. That is, we must learn to yield to the desire of our spirit, even when our flesh is moving in the opposite direction. Jesus said the *"spirit indeed is willing, but the flesh is weak."* (Matt. 26:41) As we give ourselves to be available to the Lord for prayer, we discover just how weak the flesh is. Our 'old man' cannot keep up and maintain what is needed for a mature and disciplined life, especially in regards to prayer.

Our flesh (the old man) is governed by the law of sin and is contrary to the things of the Holy Spirit. (Rom. 7:15-18;

Gal. 5:17) It is self-focused and only seeks self-gratification. We will have this old man to deal with until we put it *completely* off at death or at the second coming of Christ.

However, as we study the Scriptures, we discover that the Lord has given us the power to put to death the old man while we are walking in this life. That is, we can walk free from its influence as we yield to the power of the cross and identify with our Lord's death and life. Through faith, we reckon ourselves (our old man) dead unto sin and our new man alive unto God. (Rom 6:6,11,13) When we do, the Holy Spirit performs the putting down of our flesh along with its deeds and empowers us to move out in freedom to perform the desires of our new heart.

At the new birth, we become a new person—a new creation whereby old things have passed away, and all things have become new. (2Cor. 5:17) We are no longer *"in the flesh"* (Rom. 8:9), meaning the center of our spirit and soul has been redirected toward the things of God, and now we are *"in the Spirit."* At the core of our heart, we only desire to please the Lord and do his will. While this fact remains, we still face the *pull of the world* and the *influences of our old life* against our new life in Christ. Through the Holy Spirit, we identify with the Cross of Jesus on a daily basis throughout life, and *"put to death"* or *"mortify"* the ways and impulse of the *"old man"* that constantly attempts to regain control of our life. This is why Scriptures speak of our crucifixion with Christ as a *past* event that has already happened (Rom. 6:6; Gal. 5:25; Col. 3:9,10), and a *present* ongoing need. (Rom.

6:11; Col. 3:5,12,14) We have died, *and* we still need to put to death the old man—both are true!

As we learn the steps of the reckoning our old man to death, we experience the actions of disciplining ourselves to obey the call to prayer. Through the power of the Holy Spirit, we commit ourselves to spending time with the Lord in prayer, not in our strength but his. Throughout this stage of discipline, we also come face-to-face with the resistance of the flesh (old man), but we also learn the spiritual practice of dealing with it through the cross. We discover that it is not our commitment to prayer that keeps us going, but rather our yielding to the Holy Spirit's guidance and power. *The Holy Spirit is the source of our strength and commitment to pray.*

During this time of discipline, prayer slowly moves from a hit-and-miss practice to a lifestyle. It becomes as normal to us as a morning cup of coffee. This will not happen overnight, but it will come about when we begin to thoroughly understand our inability to walk victoriously apart from a life of prayer or God's strength.

DELIGHT

The final stage we experience in prayer is one which I call *delight*. This is the place where prayer becomes as much a practice in our life as breathing. We long to spend time with the Lord and refuse to bump our prayer time for any activity or thing. Our desire to pray has gone through the discipline stage and now has become a permanent and non-negotiable part of our walk with Christ.

It is in this delight stage that we learn the dynamics of *"praying without ceasing."* (1Thes. 5:17) Prayer is no longer just a time set aside for making requests to the Lord, but it has become our *lifestyle* and is continually dripping from our lips on behalf of others and ourself.

The beauty of this stage is that prayer is no longer a chore or job—it is a delight! We cannot see ourselves living or functioning without it. We no longer see prayer as something we should do or want to do; now it is something we thrive to do and *will not do without.*

This delight stage is a vital part of praying in the Spirit because our efforts and work have been taken out of the dynamics of our prayer time. We have become vessels in the Lord's hands for the Holy Spirit to pray in and through. We now experience being putty in the hands of God. In short, we learn to let God pray through us!

Co-Laborers with Christ

Whenever we enter this *delight* stage, we begin to grasp the practice of being a co-laborer with Christ. (1Cor. 3:9; 2Cor. 6:1; Col. 1:29; Gal. 2:20) This co-laboring is not our work coupled together with God's work. Instead, it is our yielding to his grace and allowing the Holy Spirit to be the engine, motivation, and momentum behind and through all of our doings—including prayer! We learn to get *out of the way* and allow the Lord the rightful place as Master of our life and walk. In this, we experience walking in the Lordship of Christ. We do what he says, when he says, the way he says, and through the power of the Holy Spirit.

My only desire throughout this book is for believers to enter this place of *delight in prayer*. It takes the effort and struggle of the flesh out of our commitment to pray. Discovering this hidden strength from the Holy Spirit compels us away from our efforts and into the efforts of Christ. It destroys the monotonous and boring labor which most believers experience when trying to pray.

Once we experience this stage of delight, our prayer life will *never* be the same.

Prayer:

Father, guide us through the stages of prayer that we may discover Your power in prayer. As we give ourselves to the discipline of prayer we long for the time when it moves into the delight, and we experience the joyful obedience of spending time with You. Reveal the power of the Holy Spirit to us that we may fulfill Your plan to use us in prayer. In Your name, Amen!

Chapter 5

All Prayer In The Spirit

"Praying always with all prayer and supplication in the Spirit..." (Eph. 6:18)

"...building up yourselves in your most holy faith and praying in the Holy Spirit." (Jude 20, ESV)

Before we turn our attention on the call to offer *all our prayers in the Spirit*, let's review the role that the Scriptures play. The Bible must be the basis and final authority of every discipline in the believer's life. God has given the Church the roadmap for navigating through the various minefields of doctrine, life, and experience. In other words, we must allow the truth of the Scriptures to have the authority to determine the accuracy and legitimacy of any claim. We must not interpret the Word through our experiences. Instead, we must use the Word to interpret and judge our experiences. There are many people having spiritual experiences and calling them encounters with God. However, many are either false, self-prompted, or demonic. We must learn the difference.[9]

Through the Word we have a safety net to protect us from foreign experiences. We do not have to be afraid of becoming deceived by supernatural experiences as long as we judge and discern each one *before* we accept them as authentic. Every intimate encounter with the Lord is a spiritual experience, and most experiences take place in the quiet time of prayer and meditation.

Now, let's look at what it means for *all our prayers* to be *in the Spirit.* Some of the types of prayers mentioned by Paul in the first letter to Timothy are supplications, intercessions, and giving of thanks. (1Tim. 2:1) Other verses in Scripture mention additional types of prayer; the prayer of faith, prayer of agreement, and praying in tongues. (We will explain the meaning of the different kinds of prayer in the next chapter.)

The apostle Paul instructs us that *all* of our prayers are to be *in the Spirit*. (Eph. 6:18) Therefore, we start off with one key and foundational truth—all the *different kinds* of prayer are to be *in the Spirit.* It does not matter whether it is the prayer of faith or the prayer of intercession, it is supposed to be *in the Spirit*. Because all prayer is to be in the Spirit, we know this cannot mean "in tongues" as taught in some

---

[9] Please see my book, *"Trying the Spirits"* to understand how to discern between true and false spiritual experiences.

Christian groups. If prayer in the Spirit means prayer "in tongues," how would we know whether we were praying the prayer of faith, intercession, supplication, or the prayer of agreement? See the dilemma?

According to the apostle Paul, when a person prays in tongues, no one understands him. (1Cor. 14:2) Unless the Lord gives the interpretation of the prayer, the man praying in tongues does not even know what he is praying or saying. His mind is unfruitful concerning the content of his prayer. (1Cor. 14:14) The person speaking in an unknown tongue is *responsible* for praying that *he receives* the interpretation (1Cor. 14:13) or for knowing there are believers present who have the gift of interpretation. If no one is present who has the gift of interpretation, and the person with the gift of tongues does not have the interpretation, then he must be silent before the church and simply speak to himself and to God. (1Cor. 14:28)[10]

Because of this we must understand that Paul's command to offer all prayer in the Spirit has a *deeper meaning* than just praying in tongues. (We will explain praying in tongues in Chapter 9.) When we realize that praying in the Spirit *does not* mean in tongues, we are left with the question, "What is it?" Let's begin establishing some foundational principles to help us understand praying in the Spirit.

---

[10] If believers with the gift of tongues adhered to Paul's guideline concerning the restriction and limitation of using the gift of tongues in public meetings, they would probably garner more respect from believers who do not have or understand this gift.

The Holy Spirit's Work in Prayer

The Scriptures teach us that the Holy Spirit reveals the deep things of God to the saints. Look at this passage from the Apostle Paul.

> *"But, as it is written, "What no eye has seen, nor ear heard, nor the heart of man imagined, what God has prepared for those who love him"—these things God has revealed to us through the Spirit. For the Spirit searches everything, even the depths of God. For who knows a person's thoughts except the spirit of that person, which is in him? So also no one comprehends the thoughts of God except the Spirit of God. Now we have received not the spirit of the world, but the Spirit who is from God, that we might understand the things freely given us by God." (1Cor. 2:9-12, ESV)*

Sometimes the will of God is difficult to understand because he always beholds the past, present, and future in the *now*. When we allow the Holy Spirit to show us God's will, we are receiving the *mind of the Spirit,* which cannot be contrary to the Father's perfect will. The only thing the Holy Spirit is going to reveal to us is the will of God.

The Holy Spirit does not speak or promote himself. He will only speak that which he hears from the Father and the Son. (John 16:13-15) So, if we are praying what the Holy Spirit reveals to us, we will have assurance that we are praying *the will of God.*

Remember this: *we cannot successfully pray without the Holy Spirit.* He not only leads us to pray, but he also shows us *how* and *what to pray*. It is easy for young believers to feel that they know how and what to pray, especially after the Lord answers some of their prayers. However, in order to be genuinely effective in prayer, we must maintain a *mature* attitude of realizing our *inability* and *weakness*.

> *"Likewise the Spirit helps us in our weakness. For we do not know what to pray for as we ought, but the Spirit himself intercedes for us..." (Rom. 8:26, ESV)*

We must yield to the work of the Holy Spirit by allowing him to operate in *his place* in our prayer life. Our *weakness* in prayer is that we do not know what or how to pray. Our honest and humble confession of our weakness in prayer will allow us to stand in a position of authority and power when we pray. In humility, we discover that *prayer is not about us flexing our spiritual muscles but about letting the Holy Spirit flex his.*

How does the Holy Spirit help our weakness in prayer? By making intercession for us and through us. The Holy Spirit's intercession is different from the intercession of Christ. Whereas Jesus brings our prayer to the Father, the Holy Spirit brings *to the believer* the kind of prayer that will be accepted by the Father. We must grasp this truth—our prayers should *originate* with the Father. (We will expound on this in the chapter about Ezekiel's Wheel.) The Father births a prayer in our heart by the Holy Spirit. Then we offer the prayer back to the Father through Jesus. Because of God's marvelous grace and the ministry of the Holy Spirit, we get in on the work of Christ through prayer. Think of it; we get to kneel down and join the Lord in prayer!

Look carefully as Paul teaches us about one of the operations of the Holy Spirit to the believer.

> *"These things God has revealed to us through the Spirit. For the Spirit searches everything, even the depths of God. Now we have received not the spirit of the world, but the Spirit who is from God, that we might understand the things freely given us by God." (1Cor. 2:10,12, ESV)*

The Holy Spirit *reveals the will of God* to believers so that we may pray according to the Father's will. The Holy Spirit does this because he knows that the prayers which originate from the Father will have the desire and intention of God's best for us. The prayers that the Holy Spirit reveals to us will be the Father's will. When we pray this way, we can have the fullest confidence that God hears our prayers and will answer them.

> *"And this is the confidence that we have toward him, that if we ask anything according to his will he hears us. And if we know that he hears us in whatever we ask, we know that we have the requests that we have asked of him." (1Jn. 5:14-15, ESV)*

If we do not get personal guidance from the Holy Spirit concerning the issue we are praying about, we should consider whether we are ahead of God's timing or if there is a missing element the Lord wants to unfold before revealing His will to us. We know that the Scriptures reveal the mind of the Lord concerning most things; however, there are many things we face in life which the Scriptures do not address. We need to get the mind of the Lord concerning those issues in prayer through the guidance of the Holy Spirit. A danger here is when a believer *cherry picks* a verse out of context and attempts to apply it to their personal situation when it does not apply.

An example of *cherry picking* would be for someone to use the verse, *"with His stripes we are healed"* (Isa. 53:5; 1Pet. 2:24) and try to make it an absolute promise of healing for *every* sickness or infirmity *in this life*. Paul did not lack faith concerning his affliction, and yet the Lord did not heal him. (2Cor. 12:8-10) Instead, God used the affliction to reveal and accomplish a *higher purpose* in Paul's suffering.

We all have witnessed many godly and faithful believers who have died because the Lord did not heal them from a terminal sickness. We can certainly pray for healing *unless* the Lord reveals to us a deeper or higher purpose that he is accomplishing through our affliction. Moreover, we know that ultimately, perfect and complete healing will belong to all of God's children in the resurrection.

We say we want to do the will of God. How about the will of God in prayer? The Lord calls us to pray without ceasing because through prayer we find strength for our soul and closeness to God's heart. Our prayer life will avail when we learn to offer them according to God's will.

When we pray in agreement with God's will, our prayers will build up our *"most holy faith."* (Jude 20) This building up takes place because as we pray the revealed will of God, we have an assurance that the Lord grants our request. When we know the Holy Spirit is prompting our prayer and guiding us in what and how to pray, we have *confidence* that we will receive our petition.

Over the years, many sincere believers have asked me: "Since God already knows all my needs, do we have to spend time asking? Since he knows what is best, won't he just do it?" This question usually arises from the following verse.

> *"...for your Father knows what you need <u>before you ask him</u>." (Matt. 6:8, ESV)*

The Lord did not teach us this to prevent us from praying by making it appear as an unnecessary exercise. Instead, he instructed us to seek the leading of the Holy Spirit in prayer. The flesh is always fighting to promote its desires, and the first order of business is for us to *"put off"* or *"mortify"* every desire which is in conflict with God's will. (Eph. 4:22; Col. 3:5) The *putting off* our carnal desires is only accomplished through the work of the Holy Spirit as we identify and appropriate Chris's death as our own. (Rom. 6:11)

Since the Lord already knows our needs, we can have confidence in the leading of the Holy Spirit, as he reveals the Father's plan for our life. The Lord does not grant our needs simply because he already knows them. Instead, he reveals them to us so that we can offer them to prayer. Although he knows our needs, he has chosen to include us in the petitions of prayer by calling us to make our requests in faith.

> *"Ask, and it shall be given you; seek, and ye shall find; knock, and it shall be opened unto you:" (Matt. 7:7)*

If we do not ask, we will not receive. If we do not seek, we will not find. If we do not knock, it will not be opened unto us. Truly, we have not, because we ask not. (Jas. 4:2) God's sovereignty and omniscience are not excuses for our lack of prayer. Instead, they should build our desire to seek the Holy Spirit's direction in prayer. There are many things the Lord desires to do in our life, and our lack of prayer can hinder him from accomplishing them. In the grand scheme of life, the Lord calls us to participate with him as a co-laborers in prayer.

The Lord has given us the key to turn and unlock the things of heaven. Let us be faithful to use it. The key is *prayer.* However, let us be careful never to make prayer a mechanical, lifeless, and sacerdotal exercise of the human will. Let us embrace it as a Spirit-directed and empowered discipline of our Christian walk. Prayer is one of the highest privileges for us as God's children. It calls us to embrace the responsibility to lay ourselves before God and surrender to the leadership of the Holy Spirit.

The Lord has chosen to use our prayers in His activity upon earth. One of the great mysteries of the ages is how the Everlasting, Omniscient and All-Powerful God has chosen to limit many things on this earth to the faith of His children. We *limit* the Lord and are guilty of sin when we fail to pray. (Psa. 78:41; 1Sam. 12:23)

Let each one of us begin to call on the Lord in prayer; not for the goal to get our carnal desires, but for the purpose of asking God to mold us into the likeness of Jesus Christ. Only the prayers we submit to the Lordship of Christ will carry eternal value. These are the prayers offered *in the Spirit* —or as we have seen—according to the will of God.

Prayer:

Father, we give your Spirit the free course He desires in our prayer life. Help us to understand that, by Your Spirit, you give us the form of prayer, in order to grant unto us the substance of the prayer. In Jesus precious name, Amen!

Chapter 6

Different Seasons of Prayer

"Praying always with all prayer and supplication in the Spirit..." (Eph. 6:18)

When we do a study on prayer, we soon discover there are many different *kinds* of prayer. Life also teaches this to us through the different experiences we face. As we continue to explore prayer, we also discover there are different *seasons* of prayer. This word *"always"* (Greek, *kairō*) means "time or season." When we understand the various seasons of prayer, we gain the insight to help us move into maturity in our prayer life, and this will help direct us toward *praying in the Spirit*.

Think of a season as the circumstances surrounding us at any given time. Each of the different seasons will prompt us to learn about the various kinds of prayer that *fit the season.* Just as wearing summer shorts and flip-flops do not fit a wintry season, certain kinds of prayer will not fit into every season. Different seasons call for different kinds of prayer, and the Holy Spirit is given to us to help discern the season we are in and the appropriate kind of prayer that corresponds to it.

In this chapter, we will see the *connection* between the season and the kind of prayer. However, it is essential to understand that regardless of the kind of prayer we engage in, *all* of them are to be *in the Spirit.* Let's take a quick look at the different kinds of prayer, along with the corresponding season for the prayer. As we look at these, pay close attention to the fact that each kind of prayer belongs to a *unique season.*

Different Kinds of Prayer for Different Seasons

Prayer of Repentance

If the *season* is that a person is lost or backslidden, the appropriate kind of prayer is the prayer of repentance. The prayer of repentance falls under two categories. The *first* category concerns the person who has not surrendered to Jesus as their personal Lord and Savior. This person does not have the privilege of intimate communion with God through prayer. He must first recognize his need for Christ and offer the prayer of repentance. *At times*, the Lord will answer a desperate cry from an unbeliever in order to reveal his mercy to them and bring them to salvation in Christ. He sees their heart and knows whether they are serious in their prayer. However, as a whole and a general rule, prayer is the privilege of believers, not for unbelievers. This is why a lot of *professing* Christians do not see the need for prayer, because when they pray nothing happens. However, the problem is not the Lord; the problem is their need to receive the new birth in Christ. The Lord does not hear and respond to the common prayers of sinners or non-Christians. (Jn. 9:31; Psa. 66:18) Salvation in Jesus is needed for intimate fellowship with God. (Acts 3:19)

The *second* category for the prayer of repentance concerns the Christian. If a genuine believer is aware of known sin in his life, he is out of fellowship with the Lord. His prayers will be hindered until he repents of his transgressions. (1Jn. 1:9; 2:1-2) If we allow *known sin* to stand between God and us, this hinders our spiritual ears from knowing the mind of the Spirit on anything except repentance. We may know principles of truth based on past experiences or our knowledge of Scripture, but we will not have the fresh illumination and guidance of the Holy Spirit. (Isa. 59:1-2) When we have *known and unrepentant sin* in our life, if we try to offer any other kind of prayer except repentance, even the prayers that we offer are counted as sin. (Pro. 28:9; Psa. 109:7)

We must not act presumptuously toward the Lord by neglecting the grace of repentance in our life. Keeping our sins confessed up to date is crucial if we are to enjoy constant communion and unbroken intimacy with Jesus. Repentance is not an ugly word—it is our path to remain and enjoy intimate fellowship with Christ. As Christians, we must be *quick to repent* in order to maintain a position of spiritual authority in prayer.

Prayer of Consecration

If the *season* we are facing involves affliction, persecution, or hardship, and the Lord wants us to *endure* through it, the kind of prayer would be the prayer of consecration. (Mk. 14:36; Psa. 30:7) In this prayer, we face the circumstances which are before us in the strength of the Lord so that the character of Jesus may be wrought in us. This is a season that helps to conform us into the image of Christ. (Rom. 8:18, 28-29)

Through these trials, we are compelled to grow up, to discover deep truths about God, and identify with the pains of our fellow man. The word *"mountain"* in this prayer of Psalm 30:7 (and implied in Jesus' garden prayer) has nothing to do with direct confrontation with the powers of darkness. Even though Satan may be behind it, our mountain refers to trying circumstances and tribulation. [i.e. persecution, rejection of man, false accusation, etc. (1Pet. 2:19-23; 4:12-16,19)] The prayer of consecration involves submitting to the will of God for a *higher purpose*. It does not mean submitting to attacks from the powers of darkness.

During these seasons of endurance, we discover the power of God's grace to keep us through the storms. (Isa. 43:2) It can be hard to see it at the time, but these trials of suffering work many good and spiritual qualities into our life. (1Pet. 5:10) Like coal turns into diamonds when placed under extreme pressure, our life matures into spiritual treasures when we faithfully endure affliction in the grace of our Lord.

Prayer of Faith

If the *season* we are facing is a spiritual mountain which the Lord says to remove, the kind of prayer would be the prayer of faith. (Mk. 11:23) An important distinction for us to realize is that *all prayer* is to be done *in faith.* Praying in faith is vital to every prayer because faith is our confident assurance that God hears us. But here we are talking about a specific prayer which we will call the *prayer of faith* as indicated by the phrase *"shall not doubt...but shall believe."* This kind of prayer is different.

The prayer *of faith* is an assurance from God for us to trust him for the removal of a hinderance which at the time does not serve his highest purpose in our life. This could include sickness, circumstances or barriers of resistance in which the Lord *gives us a word* concerning our need to look to him for their removal. This prayer is usually undergirded by a gift of faith granted from the Lord concerning the issue at hand.

Prayer of Agreement

If the *season* is to bind or loose the powers of darkness, the kind of prayer would be the prayer of agreement. (Matt. 18:18-20) In its central context, this prayer of agreement belongs to the practice of restorative church discipline. The passage of Matthew 18:15-20 teaches us the basic principles for handling sin between believers. However, the prayer of agreement we are looking at is a little different.

When the Lord desires us to pray with another believer for the combining of our faith and spirit, we use the prayer of agreement. Many times we may feel powerless against some circumstances when we try to stand alone. I'm convinced that during these times our Chief Shepherd is calling us into integration with other believers for our spiritual growth. The Lord wants believers to spend time together in fellowship and prayers. (Acts 1:14; 2:1, 42; Deut. 32:30)

It is important for us to understand that the phrases *"removing the mountain"* and *"binding or loosening"* may be interchangeably used in both the prayer of faith and the prayer of agreement. (Note that in Matt. 17:14-21, the mountain to be removed was the loosening of a demon from a little boy.) The prayer of faith can be offered individually (Mk. 11:23-24) or corporately (Jas. 5:14-15).

The prayer of agreement can *only* be offered by more than one and deals with binding and loosening in the spiritual realm. However, keep in mind that binding/ loosening can be done individually as pointed out above (Matt. 16:19; Jas. 4:7), as well as corporately through the prayer of agreement. (Matt. 18:18-19) The prayer of agreement seems to be the type of prayer our Lord uses to teach us to *depend* upon each other in the body of Christ. Individually we can chase a thousand enemies, but with two praying in agreement, we can put ten thousand enemies to flight. (Deut. 32:30)

Let me elaborate a little on the difference between binding and loosening. Several times while I have been sharing the Word in various churches, Satan has sent one of his messengers to hinder the work of God. Recognizing his tactics, the leaders of the church and I would gather together to offer the prayer of agreement. We joined in unity to *bind the spirit* that was operating through a person, and prayed against them interrupting the service.

I have seen the Lord shut the mouth of the lions on many occasions. If a person who came to disrupt the service did not desire deliverance, we would bind the spirit from manifesting or showing out. The enemy loves to draw attention to himself to remove the focus away from the gospel. Satan loves to *show out*, and God just wants to *show up*.

On the other side of this is loosening. This is the act of removing the spirits of darkness from a person (deliverance) or place. I remember a time when a fellow brother and I held a Bible school at a church every week. This church was under a lot of demonic warfare, and it was evident when the believers came to the school because they were always downcast and depressed. Therefore, this brother and I started arriving early at the church, before anyone else. We would sing praises to the Lord and pray to dismiss every spirit except the Holy Spirit from the premises. The people in the school would come in, unaware of what we had done, and immediately experience freedom and joy. We had loosed the powers of the enemy from the location. We continued doing this throughout the remainder of the school and never faced that same oppression again.

Prayer of Supplication

If the *season* is to petition the Lord concerning our need, the kind of prayer we offer is the prayer of supplication. (1Tim. 2:1; Phil. 4:6) The beauty, need, and importance of this prayer seems lost as a result of the reaction against the carnal "bless me" messages from the 'Word of Faith' theology. Our desire should be to restore this prayer of supplication to its proper role in our life. If we *consciously* allow the Holy Spirit to guide us concerning what to pray, our supplication will rise beyond our fleshly wants and come from the cry of the Holy Spirit for our true spiritual *need*.

I'm not implying that a Spirit-led prayer of supplication will not involve physical needs. However, even our physical needs will always involve spiritual and eternal purposes. Through prayer, the Lord is continually doing many things on many levels—and most of them we do not know about. This is one reason we should trust the Holy Spirit's guidance in prayer. When our prayer of supplication is Spirit-led, we are praying the Lord's desire for the *totality* of our life—physical and spiritual.

Prayer of Intercession

If the *season* is to go to the Lord and stand in the gap on behalf of someone else, the kind of prayer we offer is the prayer of intercession. (1Tim. 2:1) This type of prayer incorporates two levels.

First, we may offer the prayer of intercession to present a need we are aware of for someone else. We could call this offering *supplication on behalf of another.* This type of intercession is easily recognizable by listening to and engaging with people in everyday life. We hear their needs, discern the Spirit's leading concerning them, and offer petitions to the Lord on their behalf.

Second, we may stand in the gap for someone *until* the Lord shows us their need in order to make a petition to God on their behalf. This requires a sacrifice of time as we make our lives available to pray for them without any prior knowledge of their need. The only knowledge of their need we have is that we know we have a *burden to pray for them*. At times, we may know whom we are praying for, but the nature of this second level is that *we do not know what we are to pray*. This level of intercession will sometimes lead to prayer in tongues (if a person has that gift), or groanings in the Spirit. If it does lead into prayer in tongues or groanings in the Spirit, many times we will never know what we have prayed. We *may* know for whom we are praying while leaving the *knowledge of the substance* of the prayer to God alone.

Prayer of Thanksgiving

If the *season* is to give thanks (this should be a constant season in our life), then the kind of prayer would be the prayer of thanksgiving. (1Tim. 2:1; 1Thes. 5:18; Eph. 5:20;

Col. 3:17) If our heart does not have a constant disposition toward thankfulness, we need to go to prayer and find out our sin. Checking to see if our heart is thankful is a good litmus test for evaluating our trust and genuine dependence upon Jesus. *Unthankfulness is an earmark of murmuring and unbelief.* We must not take a casual attitude toward any murmuring in our life, for it always leads to some form of disobedience. (Psa. 106:25) And this, in turn, leads to a loss of power in prayer.

Praying in Tongues or Groaning in the Spirit

Though these are two different kinds of prayer, it is easier to discuss them together. They share a common element because they involve unknown requests. If the *season* is that we know we are supposed to pray, but the Lord hasn't shown us *what* to pray, then the kind of prayer *could* be praying in tongues (1Cor. 14:2,14) or groaning in the Spirit. (Rom. 8:26-27)[11] We may know what we are praying about, but we do not know the *specifics* of the prayer. Many times this may be to safeguard the privacy of another as the Holy Spirit is not a talebearer.

Notice there are *two kinds of prayer* for this *one season.* Regardless whether or not someone has the gift of tongues

---

[11] A third option is that we are to continue to wait for the Holy Spirit to reveal to us *what to pray*.

they can pray *at least one* of the kinds of prayer needed (groanings - Rom.8:26).[12] Let's briefly discuss these two.

Praying in tongues is in the same class as the other kinds of prayer because the person praying *vocalizes the words* which are being prayed. Prayer in tongues is praying in an unknown and unlearned language that has been given by the Holy Spirit. The prayer is unknown to the one praying unless the Lord reveals it to them. Usually, a prayer in tongues remains unknown to man—and known only by God.

"Groaning" in the Spirit is the kind of prayer that is entirely the work of the Holy Spirit *through* the believer. It is independent of the vocalization of any words or syllables—known or unknown. The Holy Spirit produces this *cry of the heart* in the innermost part of our being. This cry may or may not produce sounds, but there will be no words. *This is the deepest form of any prayer.*

Someone may ask, "Since groaning in the Spirit is all the work of the Holy Spirit, why doesn't the Lord just go ahead and perform His will apart from our involvement? Why does he put us through this type of pain?" I believe there are two main reasons. *First,* He has placed the earthly responsibility of His kingdom into our hands. (Matt. 16:19; 18:18-20) The Lord, in his sovereign work and plan, has chosen to include the prayers of his children as an essential part of his work

---

[12] Contrary to the teaching among some groups, this is one reason why the gift of tongues *does not* give any believer a special ability in prayer or intimacy with Christ. Those who do not have the gift of tongues are still candidates for God to use with groaning in the Spirit.

among men. May we remain faithful and never limit Him. (Psa. 78:41) He has not made us robots or potted plants—we are his friends. (Jn. 15:15)

Second, this kind of prayer also does a *work in us.* Sometimes, if we knew what we were praying, we might not ask it. The will and plan of God can seem scary at times. Groaning in the Spirit presses us beyond our own understanding and wisdom, and into the mind and wisdom of God. Though we will not know the specifics of our groaning in the Spirit, the agony of this level of intercession will transform and lead us into a more settled spiritual life of prayer. The Apostle Paul told the Galatians that he travailed in prayers for their maturity. (Gal. 4:19) God can accomplish more in our hearts through the groaning of the Holy Spirit than all the words we can muster up.

Groaning is a deep sense of concern and identification with the person we are praying for. We take on their burden, but it is too deep for words. We simply feel the deep pull and cry of the Holy Spirit within the center of our being. We become a prayer vessel for God.

Summary

Throughout this chapter, we have examined nine different kinds of prayer:

1. Prayer of Repentance
2. Prayer of Consecration

3. Prayer of Faith
4. Prayer of Agreement
5. Prayer of Supplication
6. Prayer of Intercession
7. Prayer of Thanksgiving
8. Prayer of Tongues
9. Prayer of Groaning in the Spirit

**We will look at the prayer of tongues and groaning in the Spirit in more detail in Chapter 9.

Conclusion

Looking at the different *seasons* of prayer shows us that praying the right kind of prayer is extremely vital to our walk with Christ. The reason many believers do not get their prayers answered is because they do not pray the right kind of prayer for the season which they are in. Too many times, we try to pray the kind of prayer we want *rather than* the kind of prayer the Lord knows we need. This is where the Holy Spirit comes in concerning prayer. He has been given to us to *guide us* into understanding. He will not lead us to pray contrary to the will of God in any situation of our life. He alone knows the season we are in and desires to lead us to pray the corresponding prayer with it.

Jesus said the Holy Spirit would not speak from his own authority, but only what he hears from the Son. (Jn. 16:12-15) Our responsibility in prayer is to discern the mind of the Spirit concerning our situation or season, knowing what the Holy Spirit shows us will not be contrary to the will of the Father. Apart from God, we do not know how to pray; likewise, apart from the Holy Spirit's work, we do not know—in the deepest sense—the season we are facing. Therefore, let us *consciously* seek to the Holy Spirit's guidance in our prayer life.

Prayer:

Oh Lord, I ask that You would deliver me from trying to get You involved in my prayers. Instead, teach me to get involved in Your prayers that Your eternal purpose may be fulfilled as I go through the seasons of life in my walk with You. In Your name, Amen!

Chapter 7

Abba, Father

"And he said, Abba, Father, all things are possible for you. Remove this cup from me. Yet not what I will, but what you will." (Mk. 14:36, ESV)

The will of God; how wonderful we think it is. That is, unless it is not what we want it to be. As the clay, we must be foolish to think we can say to the potter, "Do it this way." In an age when almost all businesses, from banks to fast food outlets, promise to do it our way, the Lord is still saying, *"I am the way."* (Jn.14:6) Perhaps an easy and simple way of defining praying in the Spirit would be *praying God's way.*

Let us recall the words of Jesus in the garden of Gethsemane. (Mk. 14:36) During His prayer, He cried out, *"Abba, Father."* The Aramaic word "Abba" has the same meaning as when a young child cries "da-da." (Daddy) How helpless this sounds to us as we pray, but oh how beautiful it must sound to the Father when we come to the end of our strength and helplessly cry out to him. We must surrender and depend upon the will of God the same way a young child depends upon his parents.

A young child cannot change his circumstances even if he wants to, and *neither* can we. We must humble ourselves and submit to our heavenly Father in all circumstances. How? By laying down all actions that are independent of God's leadership. Even though God has given us the right to act independently if we choose, we must freely surrender our rights back to him. This is what makes our submission to the Father so precious in his sight: we submit not because we have to, but because *we have chosen to humble ourselves* to his perfect will.

HUMILITY

> *"...Truly, I say to you, unless you turn and become like children, you will never enter into the kingdom of heaven." (Matt. 18:3, ESV)*

Through humility, we receive the kingdom of God as a child, but it doesn't end there. The Lord said that true conversion will transform us into little children. This means total submission. *Humility* is one of the earmarks of true conversion. The man who places his trust in the Lord is blessed. (Psa. 34:8) When we refuse to submit to Christ in any given situation, then we are actually saying, "I do not trust you Lord; I trust my own wisdom and strength." The Lord desires to remove this attitude from our walk.

The words, *"Abba, Father,"* are used twice by the Apostle Paul to describe the work and operation of the Holy Spirit in our hearts.

> *"...God hath sent the Spirit of his Son into our hearts, crying, Abba, Father!" (Gal. 4:6, ESV)*

> *"...but you have received the Spirit of adoption as sons, by whom we cry, Abba, Father!" (Rom. 8:15, ESV)*

Notice in Galatians 4:6, it is the Holy Spirit crying in our hearts. Then in Romans 8:15, the *believer* is crying out. When we look at these two verses together, we see that the words the Holy Spirit is crying in our hearts is *what* we pray to the Father. We cannot come to the Father except through the Holy Spirit's leading. Neither can we properly pray except we do so *through* the Holy Spirit.

> *"For through him we both have access by one Spirit unto the Father." (Eph. 2:18)*

> *"No man can come to me, except the Father which hath sent me draw him..." (Jn. 6:44)*

We see it is the Holy Spirit that draws men to Christ. The Bible says the sons of God are those who are *led* by the Holy Spirit. (Rom. 8:14) Should not this also include prayer? Can a believer actually be led by the Holy Spirit in everything—including prayer? Does the Lord still speak to

His sheep? The answers to these questions are evident in Scriptures. Yes! Yes! Yes!

> *"...the sheep hear his voice: and he calleth his own sheep by name, and leadeth them out. And when he putteth forth his own sheep, he goeth before them, and the sheep follow him: for they know his voice." (Jn. 10:3-4)*

The prophet Zechariah calls the Holy Spirit, *"the spirit of grace and supplication."* (Zech. 12:10) This verse gives us insight into the ministry of the Holy Spirit concerning prayer. He reveals to us our *genuine needs*, and as we noted in an earlier chapter, *supplication* is the request of a need. The Holy Spirit points us in the direction we need to pray so that we can cry out in prayer to the Father that which only the Spirit can explain.

Paul wrote that we cannot confess that Jesus is Lord except by the Holy Spirit. (1Cor. 12:3) Oh yes, it can be said by man's own natural or religious reasoning, but if not prompted by the indwelling Spirit, it means nothing and is a powerless exercise of futility. This is why the lauded "prayer patterns" we have seen over the past couple of decades have not produced everlasting fruit. They are a repetition of man's words rather than prayers prompted by the Holy Spirit. They are the work of the flesh. Jesus spoke out against such types of prayer. (Matt. 6:6-7) We must *never* downgrade prayer to a mechanical process or formality. Jesus is alive, and the Holy Spirit lives in us; therefore, *prayer should be a living and vibrant exercise of faith.*

If the Spirit of God is not directing our prayers, then we are wasting our time and need to learn to *wait on the Lord* in prayer. Prayers which are not Spirit-led are lacking the *passion* of our heart. These types of prayers actually become an obstacle to a healthy prayer life.

> *"This people draweth nigh unto me with their mouth, and honoreth me with their lips; but their heart is far from me." (Matt. 15:8)*

In prayer, we may speak certain things that are true, but if our hearts are not engaged through the Holy Spirit, we only offer dead religious prayers. Every believer has the Holy Spirit living in them, teaching us dependance upon the Lord. Every truth of the Scriptures concerning a Christian's life is based upon our salvation in Jesus, and the ministry of the Holy Spirit. Un-regenerated men cannot participate in the promises which belong to Christians. This is why Jesus said we must be, "born again." (Jn. 3:3)

Mechanical prayers and religious formalities are the product of natural minded men who are void of the Holy Spirit. *Praying in the Spirit* is only available to those who are new creatures in Christ—born-again through faith. Those who claim to be Christians, but lack true spiritual life, create mechanical prayers in order to appear as men of faith. We must never neglect the truth that God's sheep *hear His voice* and *follow Him.* (Jn. 10:27) And it is our humility which draws Him near to us. (Jas. 4:8-10; 1Pet. 5:5-6)

The Garden of Self Denial

Jesus offer His *"Abba, Father"* prayer in the garden of Gethsemane just before his crucifixion. We say we want to experience the joy, power, and intimacy of saying "Abba, Father" in the upper room. After all, every believer desires the boldness we see in the lives of the early Christians. However, are we willing to follow Christ faithfully if it involves the suffering, pain, and humility of crying "Abba, Father" in the garden of Gethsemane? Are we willing to submit ourselves to God's glorious path for our life?

Jesus took His disciples to Gethsemane *before* He commanded them to wait for the promise of the Holy Spirit in the upper room. *Humility and surrender will always precede spiritual power and authority.* The power of Pentecost in the believer's life will be directly related to and determined by the dying to self in Gethsemane. Let us run to the garden of self-denial and humility that we may be filled with the Holy Spirit.

In the garden, we do not see our Lord praying a vain repetitive prayer like those offered by the Sadducees and Pharisees. (Matt. 6:5,7) He was diligently seeking the desire and will of the Father. We notice a change taking place in the middle of His prayer.

> *"...nevertheless not what I will, but what thou will." (Mk. 14:36)*

Are we willing to give up our hopes and self-centered desires in prayer in order to receive the Father's will? If not, we will not experience the work and ministry of the Holy Spirit in prayer. Because whether we call it "praying in the Spirit" or "praying according to God's will," it is always linked to *self-denial.*

Praying in the Spirit is not a strategy for getting our prayers answered—it is more than that. It involves a *life of submission* to the will of God. We cannot have the leading of the Spirit until we respond properly to the conviction of the Spirit in our life. We think of praying in order to walk in purity, and this is certainly true, but David said we must be pure in order to pray.

> *"Who shall ascend into the hill of the Lord? or who shall stand in his holy place? He that hath clean hands, and a pure heart; who hath not lifted up his soul unto vanity, nor sworn deceitfully. He shall receive the blessing from the Lord, and righteousness from the God of his salvation This is the generation of them that seek him, that seek thy face, 0 Jacob." (Psa. 24:3-6)*

The definition of Gethsemane sheds light on praying in the Spirit. Gethsemane means "oil press." What an appropriate name for a place of crushing! No one would deny that our Lord's prayer in the garden was in the Spirit, but do we realize that His prayer was flowing out of His life while He was in the *oil press*? The Lord Jesus was crushed in the oil press and, on the day of Pentecost, he poured out the oil on others. As we submit to God in the oil press of prayer,, submitting ourselves to God's will, we will also experience what it means to pray in the Spirit.

Modern day Pharisees will say, "That's too hard. Do we really have to pay such a price to pray in the Spirit? Can't we just name it and claim it, confess it and possess it?" The Lord Jesus is not a spiritual credit card, and He is not going to abdicate his Lordship to the fleshly desires of carnal men. Prayers will not come to pass simply because a person uses religious sounding clichés like *decree* or *proclaim* under a pretense of spiritual authority. True power in prayer is not based upon what we say, but upon the *will of God.*

> *"Who has spoken and it came to pass, unless the Lord has commanded it?" (Lam. 3:37, ESV)*

As we come to meet the Lord in Gethsemane, we experience the crushing discipline of self-denial. The Lord shows us the sinfulness of our flesh, the failure of our wisdom, and the inability of our talents. When we see these, we gladly surrender the desires of our old man and reach out to understand and embrace God's will for our life. We walk with the Lord in Gethsemane, and the crushing weight of the failure of our flesh compels us *into His strength.* The *oil press* does its work and we benefit by discovering the power of the Holy Spirit in prayer.

Some Hindrances to Praying in the Spirit

If we are not seeking and desiring a holy life, it is impossible to pray in the Spirit *until* we repent. If we harbor sin in our life, our spiritual ears become distorted from hearing the Spirit's cry in our hearts. (Isa. 59:1-3) Some of the sins that can adversely affect our spiritual ears from hearing the Spirit's cry are:

* *Anxious spirit* - this makes me susceptible to false impressions because I'm looking for anything.
* *Partiality* - keeps me from being open before the Lord; if the Lord shows me something different, I'll try to bargain with Him.
* *Preconceived ideas* - will prevent me from even asking the Lord's direction, convincing myself of what I should do.
* *Asking amiss* - prevents me, because of known sin, from being able to hear the Lord even though I may ask.
* *Non-submissive attitude* - this could also be called pride. I have already made up my mind how I am going to do something. This usually happens even though I really know down deep what the Lord desires. This will cause me to pray what I want rather than to seek the Spirit's understanding.
* *Doubt* - if I do not believe the Lord will speak to me, then I will be unable to hear his voice for lack of faith.

PRAYER IS WORK

Prayer is not a walk in the park. Neither is it a religious exercise in an attempt to manipulate the will of God. The Lord doesn't desire for it to become a mechanical religious duty that we do apart from our hunger for intimacy with him. And while prayer is the intimate meeting between us and Jesus, the Apostle Paul informed us that it is work. He compared it to laboring and travail.

> *"Epaphras, who is one of you, a servant of Christ, saluteth you, always laboring fervently for you in prayers, that you may stand perfect and complete in the will of God." (Col. 4:12)*

> *"My little children, of whom I travail in birth again until Christ be formed in you," (Gal. 4:19)*

Praying in the Spirit is a work of faith. It is essential to understand that it is *mainly* the work of the Holy Spirit *through us.*[13] This is crucial in order for us to avoid the weariness that will come if we commit to pray but only do it out of obligation instead of surrender.

We have a choice to make concerning prayer. We can pray our own will quickly, see no results and become bored and frustrated with prayer, or we can spend time in the

---

[13] We will discuss the importance of praying in the strength of the Holy Spirit in chapter 11.

presence of God, seek the mind of the Spirit that we may pray according to His will, and see our prayers answered. If we have surrendered our life to Christ in salvation, the choice is obvious, and we are in good company.

As we learn to *pray in the Spirit,* our prayer life will begin to look more like the early disciples. That is, instead of assuming what to pray, we will begin our prayers asking the Lord to teach us to pray (Lk. 11:1) and show us what to pray. (Rom. 8:26) He will answer those question for us if we are willing to search the Scriptures and spend quiet time with him in prayer.

Prayer:

Father, lead us to the garden of Gethsemane, that the Spirit's cry in our heart may be the heart cry of our prayers. Make the life we live to be like fresh oil pouring forth from the oil press of prayer. In the name of Your Son and our Savior, Jesus Christ, Amen!

Chapter 8

Paul's Rejected Prayer

"And lest I should be exalted above measure through the abundance of the revelations, there was given to me a thorn in the flesh, the messenger of Satan to buffet me, lest I should be exalted above measure. For this thing I besought the Lord thrice, that it might depart from me. And he said unto me, My grace is sufficient for thee: for my strength is made perfect in weakness. Most gladly therefore will I rather glory in my infirmities, that the power of Christ may rest upon me." (2Cor. 12:7-9)

PAUL - A MAN OF PRAYER

If there is one thing that could be said about the Apostle Paul, it is that he was a man of prayer. In most of his writings, he mentioned prayer in one way or another. Listed below are just a few examples:

"...that without ceasing I make mention of you always in my prayers." (Rom. 1:9)

"I thank my God always on your behalf..." (1Cor. 1:4)

"Now I pray to God that ye do no evil;" (2Cor. 13:7)

"My little children of whom I travail in birth again until Christ be formed in you..." (Gal. 4:19)

"Cease not to give thanks for you, making mention of you in my prayers," (Eph, 1:16)

"Always in every prayer of mine for you all making request with joy." (Phil. 1:4)

"...do not cease to pray for you..." (Col. 1:9)

"...making mention of you in our prayers;" (1Thes. 1:2)

"We are bound to thank God always for you..." (2Thes. 1:3)

"I will therefore that men pray everywhere..." (1Tim. 2:8)

"...that without ceasing I have remembrance of thee in my prayers night and day;" (2Tim. 1:3)

> *"I thank my God, making mention of thee always in my prayers," (Ph'm. 4)*

In these verses, we see Paul did not just write and teach others to pray, but he was given to prayer in its deepest sense. Is it any wonder why God used Paul to write half the New Testament and plant churches all over the Roman Empire? His example in prayer is why he could instruct believers to follow him as he followed Christ. (1Cor. 11:1)

Paul did not waste time in his life or ministry trying to please men. (Gal. 1:10) Instead, he constantly sought the face of God and desired only to follow Christ. Through prayer, Paul saw things in the Spirit which were not lawful or proper for a man to speak about in this life. (2Cor. 12:4) Who else is qualified to give us an example of a rejected prayer, but the man who taught prayer, lived prayer, and instructed us to pray *in the Spirit*?

Rejection in prayer—that is, when God says "no"—is not a failure. Instead, it is one of the guiding markers to redirect our prayers into God's will. The only failure we experience when God says "no" is if we stop there and fail to discover what is he saying "yes" to.

Paul's Thorn in the Flesh

While discussing his rejected prayer, Paul brings up an issue which has been the cause of much debate. He mentions a *"thorn in the flesh."* (2Cor. 12:7) Let's look at a couple of things regarding it. However, as we do, we should realize that a person's opinion about what the source of this thorn is does not change the fact that his prayer was *rejected.*

First, we see that Paul's prayer was not rejected because of sin. Twice in this passage he says, *"lest I should be exalted above measure."* (v.7) I have listened to popular preachers go to great lengths trying to demonstrate that Paul's thorn in the flesh and his rejected prayer was because of pride. This was always an attempt by those who hold to false teachings about prosperity, health, and healing. However, a close look shows us that the thorn in the flesh was *preventive.* God allowed it to prevent Paul from becoming lifted up in pride. The Lord allowed this thorn in Paul's flesh so that he would not succumb to pride. Through this thorn, we see God's mercy and grace extended to him as a preventive measure.

What about this thorn in the flesh. What was it? Regardless of what it was, it does not change the fact that this prayer was rejected. However, here are the four prominent thoughts concerning it.

1. Temptations from the devil
2. Paul's opposition from his adversaries
3. Some bodily pain
4. Some reoccurring physical affliction, such as eye trouble

Most Bible scholars tend to lean toward the fourth possibility. The internal evidence from the Scriptures points strongly to the fourth option that Paul had an eye condition. (Gal. 4:15; 6:11) But remember, regardless of what this thorn was, the fact remains that Paul's prayer was *rejected*.

PAUL'S REJECTED PRAYER

Paul tells us not only that he prayed, but that he prayed *three times* for the Lord to remove this thorn. (v.8) We see that being committed to prayer does not guarantee that we get the answer we want. Neither does repeating a prayer guarantee results. Praying according to the *will of God* is the definite way of getting our prayers answered. We know the Lord hears and answers us in prayer when we pray what is His will. (1Jn. 5:14-15)

Paul also tells us what he prayed. His asked the Lord to remove this thorn from him. (v.8) Of course, this would be anyone's first request. Paul offered this request because he knew the Lord could heal. However, the Lord rejected this request because he had a *higher purpose* for Paul.

The Lord's response was: *"My grace is sufficient for thee: for my strength is made perfect in weakness."* (v.9) Now we see the higher purpose the Lord had for Paul. Along with preventing him from being lifted up in pride, the Lord wanted to use this thorn to *reveal* the sufficiency of his grace. He wanted Paul to experience spiritual strength *within* this weakness. How many times have we found ourselves trying to avoid the path of suffering before us—not realizing that our experience through it would help change us more into the image of Christ? The convicting part for us is when we see Paul's submission to the will of God. (v.9) His humility and submission to the Lord's higher purpose changed his own perspective concerning the thorn in the flesh.

In our prayer life, we must realize that the Lord is accomplishing many things on several different dimensions. This is why the Holy Spirit will only reveal to us that which is the Father's highest desire for our life. As we *wait for the Holy Spirit's promptings and guidance* in prayer, let us consider all the things the Lord is doing to reveal his glory to those around us. *Prayer is not just about us!*

PAUL'S SUBMISSION TO GOD'S WILL

> *"Most gladly therefore will I rather glory in my infirmities, that the power of Christ may rest upon me." (2Cor. 12:9)*

Here, we see Paul glorying in his infirmities. He knew that in his infirmities the power of Christ would rest upon him. The will of God was for Paul to receive a greater measure of grace and have the power of Christ on him *in his infirmities*. Paul's original prayer was contrary to this, for he sought the Lord to remove the thorn. This does not mean Paul's first three requests were wrong because Paul knew the Lord was the healer. However, because he *remained open* to the guidance of the Holy Spirit in his prayers, Paul was ready to *shift* his request to fit God's plan.

Here is an important point to understand: if Paul had asked the Lord to remove the thorn again after receiving the knowledge of God's will, that prayer would have been in the flesh. Why? Because after Paul understood the will of God, any prayer request contrary to it *could not be offered in the Spirit.* If we offer prayers contrary to the *revealed will of God*, we are rejecting his Lordship and guidance in our life. However, when the Lord revealed his will, Paul submitted to it as a beautiful example of humility. If we are to be used by God, we must do the same whenever the Lord reveals a higher purpose through our situation.

Prayer:

Father, teach us to look past the normal response for our situation and to recognize the higher purpose of Your will in our lives. Help us learn to accept and submit to Your will with the same grace as the Apostle Paul. Teach us to trust Your ways when You reject our prayers, and help us realize it is always for a higher and eternal purpose when You do. In Jesus name. Amen!

Chapter 9

Praying in Tongues

"For if I pray in an unknown tongue, my spirit prayeth, but my understanding is unfruitful. What is it then? I will pray with the spirit, and I will pray with the understanding also: I will sing with the spirit, and I will sing with the understanding also." (1Cor. 14:14-15)

I realize that the topic of this chapter is a controversial subject the modern church seems to wrestle with. Theological camps can reveal a tremendous amount of scorn for those holding opposing views. Even in the early church there were problems as evidenced by the fact that tongues is the only gift that Paul (or any other writer) spends an entire chapter trying to clear up the confusion.

My desire in this chapter is to accomplish three things: *First*, to communicate the benefits of praying in tongues for those who have it. *Second*, to correct the extremes some movements have gotten into by helping to put this gift in its proper biblical role. *Third,* to help believers who do not have this gift understand that they are *not* limited in prayer. This chapter will be divided into five subdivisions. We will try to clear up some of the confusion that exists around the topic of tongues and praying in the Spirit.

PRAYING IN TONGUES IS PRAYING "WITH THE SPIRIT"

The traditional Pentecostal or Charismatic statement concerning praying in tongues is, "When a believer prays in tongues, they are praying in the Spirit." While this statement *can* be true, it would be ignoring other Scriptures to say the only way to pray in the Spirit is to pray in tongues. We clearly saw in Chapters 5 and 6 that *all the different kinds of prayer* are to be in the Spirit (Eph. 6:18), and that praying in tongues is just *one kind* of prayer. This is important: *If all prayer is to be in the Spirit, then praying in the Spirit is more than just praying in tongues.*

Paul *does not* call the use of tongues praying in the Spirit. He calls it *"praying with my spirit."* (1Cor. 14:14-16) This will clarify much of the misunderstanding concerning prayer when we realize that praying in tongues is *with our human spirit* and that praying *in the Spirit* (Holy Spirit) is praying according to the will of God. If praying in tongues is the kind of prayer to be offered based upon the season we are in, then it will be my spirit praying in the Holy Spirit because I will be doing it according to God's will. (1Cor. 14:2)

The term *praying in the Spirit* is not synonymous for praying in tongues. Praying in tongues is simply a prayer from the human spirit offered by those who have that gift. It is a prayer which by-passes human understanding (v.14), unless the Lord gives the person the interpretation of their prayer. Paul instructed believers to seek the edification of the whole body when meeting together (v.19), and not to be immature by seeking their own edification. (v.20) Again, praying in tongues is described by Paul as praying *with the spirit* (human spirit), not praying *in the Spirit.* (Holy Spirit)

Most of the rejection of this gift stems from the immature use and idolatry of it. It is easy for believers who have this gift to become lifted up in pride and wear it like a badge of spirituality. In fact, it is one of the least of all the gifts. (1Cor. 12:28-31) Like a new born babe garners the attention of the room, so this gift, if not properly understood, will create a distraction from the cross of Christ.

The gifts of tongues and interpretation are considered lower or lesser gifts because neither one is complete without the other. It takes both of these gifts operating together to equal one of the other gifts for edifying the local church. The gift of tongues cannot edify the corporate gathering *unless* there is someone present with the gift of interpretation. Likewise, the gift of interpretation is useless apart from the gift of tongues. Therefore, Paul instructs believers to desire the *best or higher gifts*. (1Cor. 12:31)

Also, to show the lesser category of the gift of tongues, Paul says that, in the church, he would rather speak five known words for instruction than ten thousand in an unknown tongue. (1Cor. 14:19) If we always seek the edification of others, we will understand the proper role and function of all the gifts—including tongues. The practice of believers coming together in a public gathering, and all who have the gift of tongues praying loudly and without any interpretation is unbiblical and extremely immature. It creates division by separating believers into two groups—those who have the gift of tongues and those who do not.

We have no account of Paul *publicly* speaking in tongues throughout his epistles or Luke's account of his ministry through the book of Acts. Yet, we know that Paul spoke in tongues frequently and more than others. (1Cor. 14:18-19) We even know he would sing and praise the Lord in tongues or *with his spirit*. (v.15) However, because of the restrictions he gave to the church we can conclude that, unless he had the interpretation, he limited these practices to his *private time* with the Lord in prayer. The genuine believers I have known over the years who had this gift used it in the same fashion as Paul.

Praying in Tongues "in the Flesh" and "in the Spirit"

All who are familiar with Full Gospel meetings know there are times when someone will speak in tongues, and it will be obvious that it is *in the flesh*. This becomes apparent when it is used for self-promotion or to appear spiritual in the presence of others In these cases, the tongue will not minister *life* for the edification of the local body. It becomes a selfish attempt to gain attention by immature or carnal believers as they use their voice to show-off.

Then there are times when a person speaks in tongues, and it is *in the Spirit.* This is obvious by the fact that it ministers *life* to the congregation and is accompanied with the gift of interpretation. By "life," I mean how every manifestation of spiritual gifts is supposed to be in the flow of the Holy Spirit and profit or *build up all* who are present. (1Cor. 12:7; 14:12, 26) What makes the difference between these two manifestations of tongues? What puts one manifestation "in the flesh" and the other "in the Spirit?"

First, we must establish that in his first letter to the Corinthians (chapters 12-14), Paul never brings up the issue of counterfeit or satanic tongues. What he does bring up is the fact that tongues (the genuine gift) can either be manifested *in order* or *out of order*. The whole issue of Chapter 14 is not over the legitimacy of tongues, but over its *proper operation.* We have already seen that the phrase "in the Spirit" means "according to the will of God" or "in total submission to the Holy Spirit." If the Holy Spirit never does anything improper, then a message in tongues that is "in the Spirit" would mean "in proper order."

On the other hand, if the tongue spoken is *out of order*, then the message is "in the flesh" because it is not in submission to the Holy Spirit. Though the tongue *may* be a genuine gift, it is "in the flesh" when used out of order.[14] *A person could use a genuine gift of tongues and at the same time cause disturbance and confusion if they exercise it out of order in a church gathering.* Also, a person with the gift of tongues can be out of order when they are privately praying if the Holy Spirit is not leading them to pray with tongues, but instead, wants them to get quiet and discern the will of God.

If the Lord is trying to lead someone to pray the prayer of supplication, having shown them what to pray for, but they *insist or presume to pray in tongues*, then they are not submitting to the will of God. Even though, the tongue *may* be legitimate, the prayer is "in the flesh." This is not to negate the fact that there are times when the person will be involved in the other kinds of prayer, and the Holy Spirit will prompt them to pray in tongues. However, if a person has understanding of what to pray, then they *should not* pray in tongues, because when they do they will not know what they are praying. (1Cor. 14:2) When this happens the person is using tongues as a badge of spirituality and taking it out of its proper operation.

Praying in the Spirit is not a kind of prayer, but it is the *only acceptable mode* of prayer. Here are several Scripture passages concerning tongues operating out of order: 1Corinthians 13:1; 14:11, 16-17, 23. Scriptures concerning

---

[14] The Elders are responsible for correcting this. They should immediately inform the person they are *out of order* and bring the focus of the meeting back into the flow of the Holy Spirit. Communication among the presbytery is essential when correction is necessary.

the proper order are as follows: 1Corinthians 14:5, 13, 19, 26-28, 33, 39-40.

IF A CHRISTIAN HAS THIS GIFT, HOW MUCH SHOULD HE PRAY IN TONGUES?

Before attempting to answer this question, let's consider a couple of things. First, not every believer gets the gift of tongues, so this question is only for those whom the Lord gives this gift to. Second, we should *always* walk and be led by the Holy Spirit and this requires us to be in submission to Him. Since the Gospel is a life of submission and dependency, the question of how much a person should pray in tongues must also relate to the revealed will of God.

We see that Paul says, *"I will pray with the spirit."* (1Cor. 14:15) This shows us that *he made the choice* to pray or sing in tongues. Remember, this is the same Paul who was willing to die in order to keep the will of God. (Acts 21:10-15) The Holy Spirit does not over-ride the free will of man. If someone appears out of control in the exercise of any gift, he is *not* under the influence of the Holy Spirit.

The Lord is our ultimate example of submission. Let us look carefully at these verses.

> *"I seek not mine own will, but the will of the Father which hath sent me." (Jn. 5:30)*

> *"For I come down from heaven, not to do mine own will, but the will of him that sent me." (Jn. 6:38)*

This is how all the gifts of the Spirit are sanctified in the believer. We give up the *independent* operation of them by giving the gift back to the Lord to be used only according to His will and for the *edification of others.* If we operate in *any gift* independent of the Father's will, then the operation of that gift is in the flesh. (This will be discussed further in the section on prompting.) Walking a Spirit-filled life means that our will must operate *with and in submission* to the will of God.

This is also true for gifts such as preaching or even giving. For example, when a person has the gift of giving (Rom. 12:6-8) and attempts to use it at an improper time during a meeting, and thereby, causing distraction and disruption, they are using their genuine gift out of order and in the flesh. Likewise, if a teacher attempts to instruct someone while in a meeting which has been set aside for prayer only, then they are functioning in the flesh. This is true concerning any spiritual gift—out of order equals in the flesh.

Let's examine two words I believe will help us understand the operation of the gift of tongues.

Prompt

The Holy Spirit is the one who prompts or directs believers to operate in the various gifts of the Spirit. However, he never prompts anyone to operate outside the order given in the Word of God. The Holy Spirit prompts us to do things decently and in order (1Cor. 14:33,40), where *counterfeit promptings* move men to do things out of order, in confusion and to promote strife. (Jas. 3:16) This is why we must be careful about receiving a genuine gift from the Lord and allowing Satan to prompt us to use it out of order. The enemy desires to turn a blessing from the Holy Spirit into confusion.

For example, if the Lord gives someone a message in tongues, the Spirit will also lead them to give it at the appropriate time. But Satan would like for him to speak it at an inappropriate time, perhaps right in the middle of an anointed and convicting teaching. In doing this, Satan throws a cross current to the flow of the service and hinders the Holy Spirit's work of convicting the hearts of the listeners. Satan will do this to bring enough distraction to prevent someone who was under conviction from coming to Christ. Remember, the same Holy Spirit who gives us a gift will also prompt (compel/lead) us how and when to use it.

It is the responsibility of the local elders to maintain respectful order and godly decorum in the church services. They must make judgments concerning the flow and intention of the Holy Spirit within the meetings of the local body. If the elders fail to exercise this responsibility, the meetings will spiral downward into confusion and pandemonium.

Liberty

The believer who has the gift of tongues can use it at his *own choice*. Look carefully at Paul's statement in these verses:

> *"Else when thou shalt bless with the spirit, how shall he that occupieth the room of the unlearned say Amen at thy giving of thanks, seeing he understandeth not what thou sayest? For thou verily givest thanks well, but the other is not edified." (1Cor. 14:16-17)*

In this passage, we see Paul addressing the Corinthian Church about some problems concerning the gift of tongues. Some persons would offer a blessing (perhaps a meal) in tongues (with the spirit), and the people in the room did not know if they should say, "Amen" as they did not understand the prayer. He says that the blessing is good, but the others are not edified. There are times when a person may have the *liberty* to pray or sing in tongues, but *should not* because of the setting or order of the meeting. Those with the gift of tongues must be sensitive to others and not use their liberty to cause confusion. (1Cor. 14:23) We must never use our liberty in Christ as an excuse to use any gift in a selfish or self-edifying way. (Gal. 5:13)

The more we mature in our walk with Christ, the more we find that the Lord calls us to give up our rights or privileges for the higher purpose of outreach and edification. (1Cor. 8:9; 9:12; 14:18-19) Because of the unknown element within the gift of tongues, those who have this gift should use prayer, discernment, and wisdom in the operation of it, and fulfill Paul's instruction for maturity.

> *"Brethren, be not children in understanding: howbeit in malice be ye children, but in understanding be men." (1Cor. 14:20)*

Every believer should seek a mature understanding of spiritual things. We must never use our liberty, rights, gifts, or privileges to cause one of God's children to stumble. (1Cor. 8:9; Rom. 14:13; Pro. 18:19) When we genuinely seek to *edify others* instead of ourself, we will find a healthy position concerning the operation of every gift—including tongues.

Now to our question: if a believer has the gift of tongues, how much should he pray in tongues? The answer is simple: *as the Lord prompts or gives the liberty to, as long as it is in biblical order.* This is the basis for Paul's lengthy discussion concerning this gift and why he placed restrictions on it. (1Cor. 14:18-28)[15] He did not want the exercise of this gift to cause others to reject Christ or confuse the message of the Gospel.

If we embrace the call to become a servant and *seek that which is best* for our brother, we will gain much wisdom in the function of the gift of tongues, as well as every other gift. We

---

[15] Some would argue that the restrictions were for a message in tongues and not for the exercise of praying or worshipping in tongues. This distinction is based upon Paul's statement about "various kinds of tongues." (1Cor. 12:10) However, Paul did not make an exception in his discourse in chapter 14. In fact, he mentions a message in tongues, prayer in tongues, and worship in tongues throughout the chapter. He was placing restrictions and guidelines upon all. (1Cor. 14:13-19, 23-28)

are called to build up others, not tear them down or cause them to stumble through seeking selfish attention.

The Purpose of Praying in Tongues

As with all the gifts of the Holy Spirit, we should be thankful for the gift of tongues which is given to *some* believers. Just because of its abuse and misuse in some churches, let us not become reactionary and equally wrong by refusing its proper role. And while Paul taught us *not to forbid* speaking with tongues, he also instructed that it must be exercised *decently and in order*. (1Cor. 14:39-40)[16] With this in mind, let's look at Scripture to see some of the benefits of praying with tongues for those who have this gift.

* *1Corinthians 14:2*, we see that tongues is speaking unto God and is beyond our human understanding. When tongues is in proper operation, the believer speaks mysteries in the spiritual realm. Sometimes the Lord reveals the prayer/message to the church through interpretation. (1Cor. 14:13)
* *1Corinthians 14:4*, we are told that praying in tongues edifies the individual. This means to "build up."
* *1Corinthians 14:15* - we see that a believer can use tongues to worship the Lord.

---

[16] This one reference from Paul's letter to the Corinthians corrects both the errors we see today—the rejection of this gift and the improper exercise of it.

With these spiritual benefits in mind, let us look at a *misunderstanding* and *improper use* of praying with tongues. Over many years of ministry, I have read many books and pamphlets on praying in tongues by leading Pentecostal and Charismatic brethren. There are two statements some make that we must contest based upon Scriptures. The phrasing may differ, but they usually state them as follows: "If you do not know what to pray, just pray in tongues and give it over to God" or "You need to pray in tongues as much as you can."

We have already answered the second statement in a previous section in this chapter. The amount of time a person prays with tongues must be submitted to the Holy Spirit. That is, we should only pray as the Holy Spirit leads, and not based upon our assumption about its benefit. The Lord has not set up a competition to see who can pray with tongues the most. As with all the gifts, tongues has its place as the Holy Spirit leads, and it is clear to anyone using discernment that most of what we see today is not led by the Holy Spirit.

But what about the first statement? Many believers are missing the Holy Spirit's desire to operate through their lives in prayer, by taking it for granted that if they do not know what to pray they should begin praying in tongues. At times, this *may* be true—if the Holy Spirit is leading the believer to pray in tongues in agreement with the season they are in. (See chapter 6) However, I've witnessed many immature believers who have this gift, attempt to *manufacture* the presence of the Lord in a prayer meeting by praying in tongues. They were actually guilty of *quenching the Holy Spirit.* Every believer, regardless of their spiritual gift, should seek to *get in the flow of the Holy Spirit* by discerning the Lord's desire in the given situation. God is not an old water pump that needs to be primed. He knows what we need and is more than willing to reveal it to us.

Those who teach believers to a) pray in tongues as much as you can, or b) pray in tongues whenever you don't know what to pray are the cause of spiritual damage in the prayer life of believers. In some Pentecostal and Charismatic camps, those who have this gift think that every time they need to pray about something, they can speak a few words in tongues and leave it to God. This is not taught in the Scriptures but is an assumption by ignorant and immature leaders. The truth is that the Lord wants every believer to depend on him, seek him, listen to him, and obey him—even in prayer. If a believer's prayer life consists of praying with tongues and leaving the prayer with God every time he does not know what to pray, he has other problems. That is, he lacks understanding of prayer and is untrained concerning the work of the Holy Spirit through prayer.

Praying in the Spirit carries many responsibilities. The main one is for us to *spend time waiting before the Lord* until he reveals his will concerning what we should pray. In many situations, we already have his will revealed in the Scriptures. However, there are other times when we do not know what to pray. The leadership of the Holy Spirit grants us confidence when we pray. (1Jn. 5:14) Waiting can be one of the hardest things to do in prayer. It requires a deep work of patience and submission. Learning to wait on the Lord offers blessings to us that go beyond simply getting directions for praying. We also get our hearts strengthened as we wait.

> *"Wait on the Lord: be of good courage, and he shall strengthen thine heart: wait, I say, on the Lord." (Psa. 27:14)*

Edification and strength do not come from praying with tongues only. They also come from waiting quietly before the Lord—and every believer can do this. Those who wait upon the Lord and look for His direction receive spiritual nourishment in due season. (Psa. 145:15) If we end our prayers and walk away from our time with God before we receive the due season of His direction, we will miss getting the spiritual meat we desire. This meat is to *know* and *do* the will of God. (Jn. 4:34)

> *"Show me thy ways, 0 Lord, teach me thy paths. Lead me in thy truth, and teach me for thou art the God of my salvation; on thee do I wait all the day." (Psa. 25:4-5)*

Let us go before our Lord and allow the Holy Spirit to lead and show us what kind of prayer to offer. Remember, praying in tongues is only *one kind* of prayer, so let us put it in its biblical place and not allow the flesh or false teaching to exalt it as a super prayer. If you have the gift of tongues, be thankful for it. However, remember that you still bear the responsibility to seek the Lord to find the mind of the Spirit. If you use tongues as a pop-off value to give your burdens to the Lord, you will remain an immature babe in Christ.

If we fail to spend quality time with God in prayer, we will miss the deep work and ministry of the Holy Spirit. The Spirit's job is to lead, guide, comfort, enable, and reveal God's will to us. In regards to the exercise and purpose of spiritual gifts, the Lord calls us to be mature in our *understanding*. (1Cor. 14:20) It is time we spend quality time with the Lord in prayer and grow up.

AM I LESS EFFECTIVE IN PRAYER IF I DO NOT HAVE THE GIFT OF TONGUES?

Consider the ministry of men such as D.L. Moody, John Wesley, George Whitefield, Andrew Murray and many others who led some of the great moves of God seen in America and other countries. And yet, they never testified to or mentioned having received the gift of tongues. With all the emphasis on tongues by some believers and churches, we do not see the work of the Holy Spirit like witnessed in the days of these men. We see a lot of activities which claim to be the move of the Holy Spirit, but many are nothing more than psychosomatic manifestations or the work of foreign spirits masquerading as the move of the Spirit.

Every great move of God has included men and women who gave themselves to prayer. The Lord moved as they prayed *in the Spirit* and got in on what God was doing rather than trying to get the Lord in on what they wanted to do. They were truly *"endued with power from on high."* (Lk. 24:49)

When a believer surrenders his life to Jesus as Lord and Savior, he is baptized with the Holy Spirit and has all of God. This is the fundamental truth of the new birth. The question is not about getting more of God, but about *letting God have more of us*. As we grow in Christ, we begin to understand the call to walk in his Lordship in every area of life. This, in turn, is a call to a deeper and more insightful surrender to the control of the Holy Spirit.

Though all believers are baptized in the Holy Spirit at salvation, there are many fillings. We should constantly seek the Lord and ask him to fill us afresh with the fulness of the Holy Spirit. We must have his strength and power in order to accomplish his work upon the earth.

We are commanded to be *"filled with the Holy Spirit."* (Eph. 5:18) Believers may describe the filling of the Holy Spirit in various ways, but the main thing is to have it. It is better for a person describe the Spirit's filling wrong and have God's power in their life, than to describe it correctly and not have it. Let us all ask the Lord to fill us afresh with the Holy Spirit, and leave the manifestation or results up to God.[17]

---

[17] Throughout the NT we see different manifestations resulting from the filling of Holy Spirit: Joy, Prophecy, Tongues, Healing, Boldness, Singing, Worship, Persuasive speech, Visions, etc. We are wise to let the Lord decide who gets what, and to stop elevating any one manifestation as proof of the Spirit's filling.

The Deepest Prayer

Remember all the different kinds of prayer: thanksgiving, supplication, intercession, consecration, prayer of faith, prayer of agreement, and praying "with the spirit" or "in tongues." All of these prayers use *our words*, whether known or unknown. However, there is a kind of prayer that is available to every believer which is *deeper than any of the above prayers*. It is the type of intercessory prayer mentioned by Paul in his letter to the Romans.

> *"...but the Spirit itself maketh intercession for us with groanings which cannot be uttered." (Rom. 8:26)*

This prayer (groaning in the Spirit) is so deep that it is not even possible to express it in *any language*, known or unknown. It is strictly the Holy Spirit crying out his desire and plan through us *without words.* In this prayer, the believer is the vessel God uses to express His will in prayer. Look at these two translations of Romans 8:26.

> *"...but the Spirit Himself goes to meet our supplication and pleads in our behalf with unspeakable yearnings and groanings too deep for utterance." (Amplified Version)*

> *"...but the Spirit himself intercedes for us with sighs too deep for words." (Revised Standard)*

Notice the expression *"too deep for words"* that Paul uses to describe this kind of prayer. The deepest form of prayer given in the Bible does not involve the use any words—*known or unknown*. It is available to all believers, whether they have the gift of tongues or not. It is so deep that even the prayer tongue, which some have received, cannot reach its depth.

Those who have engaged in this level of intercession will attest to its supremacy among the different kinds of prayer. This groaning in the Spirit is so deep that it is the only prayer that is independent of *any verbal expression*. A believer may have various levels of intercessory prayer in tongues or in their native language, but according to Paul, no prayer is as deep as those which are *beyond the expression of words.*

We see a perfect analogy of this kind of prayer in the celebration of the Feast of Tabernacles. Every day, during the feast, the High Priest would pour out water as an offering before the Lord. The water was taken from the stream of Siloah which flowed under the temple-mount. The High Priest would pour the water from upon the altar from a golden pitcher. The golden pitcher is an symbol of the believer who is walking in holiness and is a vessel *"meet for the masters use."* (2Tim. 2:20-21) The water represents the Holy Spirit. (Psa. 72:6; Isa. 44:3; Jn. 7:38-39) The High Priest represents, of course, our Lord Jesus. (Heb. 8:1) As the High Priest poured out the water, the only noise heard was the *sound of the water*—not the sound of the pitcher.

Likewise, during times of deep intercession, when Jesus (our High Priest) pours out His Spirit (the water) *through* believers (the pitcher), the *only sound* heard is the sound of the Holy Spirit crying through the believer. We become the vessel he uses to bring to pass his plan and desire. This is part of our call as His bride. We are privileged to have the Lord use us in this way, and this intercession is available to every believer. This *pouring forth* of the Holy Spirit through us is a solemn offering to the Lord upon the *altar of prayer!*

Conclusion

In closing this chapter, I would like to share a personal story concerning what the Lord taught me about prayer. Do not get caught up in thinking you must have a lot of noise in order to be effective. *Let the Holy Spirit be in charge of the tone.* In Moses' Tabernacle, the greatest amount of noise was in the inner court where the animals, bellowing and bleating, were put to death. Yet, *within the tabernacle*, this was the furthest place from the presence of God.

In the Holy Place, the dishes and snuffers could be heard every now and then. It was quieter than the inner court and a *little closer* to the Glory of God. In the Holy of Holies, it was not man, but *God who spoke* as He communed with the High Priest from above the Mercy Seat. There was no noise or sacrifice—only the Glory of God. It was the *quietest place* in the Tabernacle, but it was the place where man met the Lord face to face. God still meets us in the quietness of reflection. Just because a prayer meeting is loud does not mean the Holy Spirit is there.

"Be still, and know that I am God..." (Psa. 46:10)

Prayer:

Father, I thank You for every gift that You have given me, and now I lay them all at the foot of the cross that they may be sanctified before You. I forsake the independent use of them and pray that You use them through me according to Your Divine will. Teach me the path of submission and the power of silence in Your presence. Amen!

Chapter 10

Ezekiel's Wheel

"Now as I looked at the living creatures, I saw a wheel on the earth beside the living creatures, one for each of the four of them. As for the appearance of the wheels and their construction: their appearance was like the gleaming of beryl. And the four had the same likeness, their appearance and construction being as it were a wheel within a wheel." (Ezek. 1:15-16, ESV)

THE VISION

In the first chapter of Ezekiel, the prophet described the vision of the Glory of God that he saw by the river Chebar. Ezekiel was allowed to see into the heavens and behold God's Glory. (Ezek. 1:1), and he saw the inner workings of the Holy Spirit.

> *"...for the spirit (Holy Spirit) of the living creatures was in the wheels." (Ezek. 1:20-21; 10:17, ESV, parenthesis added for clarity)*

> *"Wherever the spirit (Holy Spirit) wanted to go, they (the wheels) went…" (Ezek 1:20 ESV, parenthesis added for clarity)*

Here, we see that the wheels move in the direction the Holy Spirit moves. As the four living creatures only move as the Holy Spirit leads and guides them, so believers should only move as the Holy Spirit moves. In this vision, we are seeing how the Kingdom of God in heaven operates. It is fully submitted to the will of God. While teaching the disciples about prayer, Jesus told them to pray:

> *"Thy Kingdom come. Thy will be done in earth, as it is in heaven." (Matt. 6:10)*

The will of God in heaven is carried out by the *movement* of the Holy Spirit. According to Jesus, the Kingdom of God on earth (the Church) should be directed and guided the same way. As believers, we should see this as a privilege. The Lord desires to guide us throughout life, especially our prayer life, by the Holy Spirit.

The next thing we should note before we explain how this vision pertains to praying *in the Spirit*, is that Ezekiel says he beheld *"one wheel upon the earth."* In this vision, Ezekiel was looking into the heavens as they were opened (Ezek. 1:1), but the wheel he saw was so big that it reached the earth. (Ezek. 1:15,18) Ezekiel sees a wheel which symbolizes the omnipresence of our Lord and touches every dimension of life and space. This is also described by David in one of his Psalms.

> *"Where shall I go from your Spirit? Or where shall I flee from your presence? If I ascend to heaven, you are there! If I make my bed in Sheol, you are there! If I take the wings of the morning and dwell in the uttermost parts of the sea, even there your hand shall lead me, and your right hand shall hold me." (Psa. 139:7-10, ESV)*

As Ezekiel looks at the wheels, he sees that they are *"full of eyes round about."* (Ezek. 1:18) This represents the infinite wisdom of the Holy Spirit who does not lead us into blind fortune. The Scriptures teach us that the eyes of the Lord run to and fro throughout all the earth and He seeks to help those who have pure hearts. (2Chr. 16:9)

Since the Holy Spirit sees and knows all things, we must come to the place of trusting his leadership in our prayers. He knows *how, when* and *for what* we should pray. This is why his work and ministry is so essential in our prayer life. Our Lord has sent us the Holy Spirit as the great comforter to *lead us* into all truth. (Jn. 16:13)

Let's look at one last thing we should consider before applying Ezekiel's vision to our prayer life.

> *"...a wheel within a wheel." (Ezek. 1:16, ESV)*

In this vision, Ezekiel sees a wheel within (in the middle of) another a wheel. Here, we see a picture of the *intercession of Christ* and the *intercession of the Holy Spirit* working together. The wheel in the middle of the wheel represents the hub or center of the wheel.[18] This center wheel is the middle point or medium from top to bottom.[19] As our mediator, Jesus is the middle point or medium of life between the Father and man, between heaven and earth.

> *"For there is one God, and there is <u>one mediator between God and men</u>, the man Christ Jesus," (I Tim. 2:5, ESV)*

Jesus is the *wheel in the middle of the wheel* or the very place (the hub) that mediates between heaven and earth. He stands alone as the great intercessor between God and man. He is our arbiter who lays hold of both God and man (Job 9:33), and our near kinsman who redeems us. (Ruth 3:12) As God, Jesus is the only begotten of the Father. As a man, he is the son of David. (Rom. 1:3-4) He is the only one who touches both God and man by having both natures in his person—divinity and humanity.

The outside wheel, or the ring, is the Holy Spirit. The Spirit's intercession is to speak what he hears, and it always glorifies the Lord Jesus. Everything the Holy Spirit leads us

---

[18] Adam Clarke's Commentary on the Holy Bible.

[19] I realize that some scholars think of the wheels as being in the form of a gyroscope and this certainly has merit. However, for our understanding of prayer I have chosen the image of a *hub* in order to illustrate the ministry and intercession of Christ in prayer.

to pray or do revolves around the hub, which is Jesus. (Jn. 16:13-14)

The Application of Ezekiel's Wheel

Let us apply Ezekiel's wheel to *praying in the Spirit.* Pay careful attention how the wheel must make *two full rotations* in order for the prayer to be complete. We will look at these principles in four steps for simplification and clarity. However, when we pray in the Spirit, it is an unbroken and continuous flow of the Holy Spirit. It will not be mechanical or feel fragmented by steps. Each step will revolve around Jesus—who is the centerpiece of prayer.

Step One

The wheel of prayer makes a half turn from heaven to earth when the Father sends the Holy Spirit to reveal to our heart the prayer we should offer. This prayer is connected with the situation or season we face. Genuine prayer *begins with God,* and because of his omniscience he knows exactly what we need. What the Holy Spirit shows and leads us to pray will be the will of God. (Rom. 8:26-27; Gal. 4:6; Rom. 8:15) This is why we must learn the truth of *waiting* on God in prayer. Not just waiting for the answer, but waiting to discover what we *should* pray.

Step Two

The wheel of prayer makes another half turn from earth to heaven when we submit to the will of God and offer to the Father the prayer revealed to us by the Holy Spirit. We will have confidence in this prayer; since it is his will we know he will answer it. (Jn. 16:23; 14:26; 1Jn. 5:14-15) We cannot fulfill this unless we listen to the Lord's voice *before* we assume what his will is. The Lord desires to teach us how to hear his voice clearly that we may be able to pray his will.

Step Three

The wheel of prayer makes another half turn from heaven to earth when the Father, through the Son, grants our petition through by the Holy Spirit. Because the Lord initiated the prayer, we know it is God's will to pray it. (Jn. 14:13-14; 15:7; 1Jn. 5:14-15)

Step Four

The wheel of prayer makes its final half turn from earth to heaven when we offer thanksgiving and worship to the Father for answering our prayer. (Eph. 5:20; 1Thes. 5:18) Sometimes our thanksgiving will be *before* we see the manifestation of the answer to our prayer. At other times, our prayer may be immediately answered. (i.e. healing, strength, etc.) However, usually our prayers include a time period between our petition and the realization of the answer. Since we have offered our prayer in the Spirit (the will of God), we should be thankful *before* we see the answer manifested because we know, *through faith*, we have what we asked. (1Jn. 5:14-15)

Faith is the substance and evidence of the answer to the prayer offered according to God's will. (Heb. 11:1) It is settled in our hearts even though we still wait for the answer to be realized. Faith gives us the certainty that God has granted our petition. Like Abraham, we *believe* God based upon his promises. We know that he *"calls into existence the things that do not exist."* (Rom. 4:17, ESV) Because God has promised them to us, they are as certain as if they were already in existence.

When we *pray in the Spirit,* we allow the Lord to begin the prayer. Then we present His prayer back to Him. Because we received a *word* from heaven, we have assurance and confidence that God will grant our petition. It is now settled in heaven and in our hearts—it is a done deal!

The Momentum of Our Prayer

The power of the Holy Spirit is supposed to be the *only momentum* of our prayers. If it is not, then we are praying "in the flesh" and attempting to use emotions or human effort as our sustaining strength. Our fleshly strength will always stop the wheel. This is why we should seek to offer all prayers *in the Spirit.*

As we have seen, there are two rotations of the wheel for each answered prayer. If any phase of prayer is missing, the wheel stops turning. If the momentum is the power of the Holy Spirit, then by God's grace the prayer wheel keeps turning.

I have often wondered if the author to the song, *"Just A Little Talk With Jesus"* had this in mind when he penned these words.

> *"Now when you feel a little* ***prayer wheel turning,***
> *And you know a little fire is burning,*
> *You will find a little* ***talk with Jesus*** *makes it right."*[20]

The ministry of the Lord Jesus in prayer is that he is our mediator. As a mediator, his ministry works two ways:

1. From party one to party two. (i.e. from the Father to the believer)
2. From party two to party one. (i.e. from the believer to the Father)

In prayer, not only does the Father desire that we talk to him, but he desires to talk to us. Prayer is a spiritual dialogue. There is no bargaining or manipulation that takes place in Spirit-filled prayers. As believers, we must *always submit* to the will of the Father in order to be effective in prayer.

One of the deepest joys of praying in the Spirit is knowing that the Lord is the one keeping the prayer wheel turning. We do not have to work it up, conjure it up, or maintain the prayer. We only have to *yield* to the ministry of

20 *"Just A Little Talk With Jesus"* by Rev. Cleavant Derricks (1910-1977)

the Holy Spirit as he prompts us concerning what or how to pray.

An Example of Praying in the Spirit

Let us look at an example from the Scriptures which demonstrates the importance and necessity of praying in the Spirit.

> *"Then Peter arose and went with them. When he was come, they brought him into the upper chamber: and all the widows stood by him weeping, and showing the coats and garments which Dorcas made, while she was with them. But Peter put them all forth, and kneeled down, and prayed, and turning him to the body said, Tabitha, arise And she opened her eyes; and when she saw Peter, she sat up. And he gave her his hand, and lifted her up, and when he had called the saints and widows, presented her alive. And it was known throughout all Joppa; and many believed in the Lord." (Acts 9:39-42)*

In this passage, we see Peter asking for all the widows to leave the upper chamber. Perhaps this was because he wanted to pray and get the mind of the Spirit without the danger of being misled or confused by hearing their emotional cries, opinions, or thoughts about Dorcas. Then, we see Peter kneeling down to pray. He did this *before* doing anything else. The passage strongly suggests that Peter was seeking God's will through prayer as he did nothing until *after* he prayed.

Notice that after Peter prayed, he turned to the body of the woman and said, *"Tabitha, arise."* From the language of the text, it appears that the Lord revealed to Peter that he desired to raise Tabitha from the dead. A gift of healing[21] was given to Peter to minister to Tabitha. Notice that Peter did not say, "Lord, please raise her up." But with certainty he said, "Tabitha, arise." What made him so certain? The wheel of Ezekiel had started turning, bringing the will of God to Peter, and he simply offered the prayer which the Holy Spirit revealed to him.

Conclusion

To close this chapter, let's look at three illustrations from the pen of King Solomon. These examples come from nature and demonstrate the cycle of our prayers when we pray *in the Spirit.*

Prayer is Like the Sun

> *"The sun rises, and the sun goes down, and hastens to the place where it rises." (Eccl. 1:5, ESV)*

Here, we see the sun going down and rising where it started. Likewise, our prayers should come down from the

[21] Raising the dead is a gift of healing and is different from resurrection. Resurrection gives the person a glorified body (only Jesus performs a resurrection), but being raised from the dead restores life to the person on a natural level. The person raised from the dead will eventually die again.

Lord and then return to him when we offer them in faith. They *start with God* and return to him when we pray.

Prayer is Like the Wind

"The wind blows to the south and goes around to the north; around and around goes the wind, and on its circuits the wind returns." (Eccl. 1:6, ESV)

Here, we see the wind whirling about *around and around.* Likewise, the Spirit is moving constantly, and we should desire to be sensitive to his faintest whisper and leading. He is always desiring to lead us into the mind and will of the Father concerning prayer. When we pray *in the Spirit,* we get into his circuits instead of trying to convince Him to get into ours.

Prayer is Like the Rivers

"All streams run to the sea, but the sea is not full; to the place where the streams flow, there they flow again." (Eccl. 1:7, ESV)

During prayer, rivers of truth will flow into our heart from the Lord. However, in order for these rivers to benefit our life, we must let them *evaporate* back to the heavens. As we spend time in the Lord's presence and allow his glory to shine upon our hearts, he will draw the rivers of prayer back into the heavens.

With these three examples, we learn that even nature teaches us the principles of *praying in the Spirit.* Prayer is the highest form of activity that we get to do as co-laborers with Christ. And when we discover the enabling grace of the Holy Spirit, prayer is no longer a dreaded activity.

Prayer:

Father, open my eyes in the Spirit that I may see Your will and my ears that I may hear Your guidance. Teach me, oh Lord, more about Your work behind the veil of Your Temple, through silence in Your presence. I invite You to be the Alpha (the beginning) and Omega (the ending) in all my prayers that I may offer them to You in the Spirit. In Jesus name, Amen!

Chapter 11

Praying in the Strength of the Holy Spirit

"Not by might, nor by power, but by my Spirit, says the Lord..." (Zech. 4:6, ESV)

Throughout this book, we have developed and shown the truth that praying *in the Spirit* is the same as praying the will of God. It is impossible to separate the two. However, while we understand this let us also realize a crucial issue. *We can verbalize the will of God in prayer and still fail to pray in the Spirit.*

If we pray the will of God *apart from* the strength of the Lord, we are not praying in the Spirit. We are only verbally rehearsing before God what He wants us to pray because prayer can not be separated from *faith* or the *strength* of the

Holy Spirit. Let's develop some principles involved along these lines of thought.

What is Prayer?

At the core of the subject of prayer, we are immediately drawn to this question, "What is Prayer?" The simplest answer involves two dimensions. *First*, prayer is talking to God. *Second*, and just as important, prayer is God talking to us.

As we saw in the vision given to the prophet Ezekiel, prayer, in its purest form, *begins with God*. Because of the unity of these two dimensions, it is correct to say that prayer involves a *dialogue* with the Lord. In the modern church, prayer has become more of a monologue, with the Christians doing all of the talking. We spend most of our time in prayer telling the Lord what we want rather than seeking him to discover what *He wants us to want.* Learning to pray in the Spirit calls us back to the *dialogue* of prayer, and back to where we find the treasures of God's plan for our life awaiting us.

Prayer is an Exercise of Faith

Our communication to God through prayer is an exercise of our faith Christian faith. Simply put, *we pray because we believe*. This is not to imply that everyone who offers a prayer has believed unto salvation or is walking in faith. Various religious people from different cultures will offer prayers with the wishful hope that God exists and hears them. For the Christian, prayer is an exercise of personal faith because of the truth that Jesus is our Lord and Savior, and we know God exists and hears us in prayer. *True Christian faith always leads to prayer, but prayer does not always lead to true Christian faith.*

Prayer is the life blood of our soul and spirit. Just as an infant desires his mother's milk for food and oxygen to breathe, every child of God desires the presence of the Lord. Prayer is our spirit crying, "Abba, Father." Apart from the simple faith of trusting in Jesus, prayer becomes an exercise of futility and pride. It takes on the form of a religious incantation rather than a heart-to-heart encounter with Christ. Without faith, prayer loses the dynamics of personal intimacy.

Only in the disposition of faith can we enter the biblical reality of prayer. For Christians, our conversation with God is more real and necessary than anything seen or heard in the world around us. Faith is the steadfast confidence and assurance that we have communion with Jesus. Apart from faith, prayer is not biblical prayer. Because, without faith, it is *impossible* to please God or to draw near to Him. (Heb. 11:6)

Prayer and the Will of God

Effective prayer is directly linked with the *knowledge* of the will of God. The focus of this book has been to help us see our need to spend *quiet time before the Lord* in order to ascertain his will before we enter into prayer requests. This, as we have seen, is how we let the Lord *initiate* our prayers so we will enter into the mind of the Spirit and pray according to the will of God. Any prayer that is outside of God's will cannot be offered in the Spirit.

Many believers try to relieve their responsibility to discover the will of God by saying, "according to your will" while praying. All of us have probably heard this in various churches we have attended. This usually happens because most believers have learned that we should offer our requests according to God's will. (1Jn. 5:14) However, the Lord never intended for it to become a *tag* we place on the end of our prayer request. Instead, we need to regain our responsibility to come into his presence, find his mind on a given matter, and then pray according to his highest purpose in that situation. Therefore, the phrase "according to God's will" is not a tag to end a prayer, but *a call to enter into prayer*.

We must discern what is the will of God in order to pray *effectively*. We must be on guard to recognize a trap Satan desires to draw us into. After we understand the will of God concerning our situation, we can pray using the terminology which describes God's will without entering into true prayer. We must take the will of God and offer it *in the strength of the Holy Spirit* and *in faith* in order to enter genuine prayer.

We face two pitfalls as the enemy attempts to sidetrack our prayers. *First*, Satan does not want us to find out God's will. He wants us to continue offering selfish prayers so our time with God becomes useless. This will eventually lead to a neglect of prayer because it becomes a waste of time. God does not respond to our carnal requests, and if we fail to understand the biblical principles of praying in the Spirit, we will think that prayer does not actually change things.

Second, after we discover God's will, Satan does not want us praying in the strength and power of the Holy Spirit. This too will make our prayers ineffective. If we do not offer our prayers in the strength of the Holy Spirit, our knowledge of the will of God has profited us nothing. The enemy hates our prayers, and he will do anything within his power to prevent us from praying in the strength of the Holy Spirit or in faith. When we only exert our efforts and and strength in prayer, we become physically weary from the toil it takes upon our body. When we learn how to *pray in the Spirit*, God becomes our strength and we stop relying on human effort in prayer.

Prayer Must be in Spirit and in Truth

Jesus said, *"God is a Spirit: and they that worship him must worship him in spirit and in truth."* (John 4:24) Prayer, in its proper function, is part of the larger scope of worship. Worship is the reverence and devotion we offer to the Lord. Christian prayer is a reverent devotion to Jesus as the risen Savior. This places prayer in the category of worship, along with obedience, reading the Bible, and singing. Without the exercise of faith, all of these practices become nothing more than the performance of a religious duty.

All dimensions of worship must be done in spirit and truth in order for them to quality as Christian worship.

Since prayer is one form of worship it would be included in this statement. Let's look at the application of how prayer is to be in the Spirit and in Truth.

Prayer in Spirit

Our prayers are to be in the Spirit. We have discussed this over and over throughout this book. Only through the ministry of the person of the Holy Spirit can we pray in the Spirit. The Holy Spirit is given to each believer in Christ as our comforter and our teacher. (Jn. 14:16; 1Jn. 2:20, 27) The Holy Spirit is always leading believers into maturity by prompting us to go deeper into the spiritual level of life. This is his realm of leadership and ministry. He is continually pleading with us to live, walk, and pray with and through his strength. God calls us to worship and pray through the strength of the Holy Spirit.

Prayer in Truth

Offering prayer in truth refers to everything we have discussed in relation to offering our prayer according to God's will. It also refers to prayer in accordance with the truth of the Bible. I know this seems obvious to most of us, but I have seen occasions when Christians said they were trusting God for things that contradicted Scriptures. They would try to claim a personal word or impression even when it was opposed to the truth of the Bible. Many times these impressions are verses from the Bible which have been taken out of context. *A verse out of context becomes a presumption and leads to error.*

Briefly stated, *praying in truth* refers first and foremost to the truth of the Bible. Second, it also involves praying what God has spoken to our hearts as a personal word through the Spirit's leading. However, the Holy Spirit's leading will *never* contradict the sound and balanced interpretation of the Scriptures.

Praying In and Through the Person of the Holy Spirit

Our prayers involve an *intimate* communion with the Holy Spirit. They connect our spirit with God's Spirit in our daily walk. This is one of the privileges of being a child of God—we can yield to the Holy Spirit for strength and power in prayer. We must never trust in our own strength or abilities. If we do, prayer will become boring, redundant, lifeless, and useless. We see this happen when believers jump on the bandwagon and follow the mechanical "prayer patterns" that cycle around every couple of years. These natural methods of prayer are usually more about getting recognition for praying than encountering God through praying. And the result is a lot of people become worn out, but never learn to pray *in the Spirit.*

The prayer ministry of the Holy Spirit in Christians will not be limited to or promoted by man's seven steps for successful prayer. The Holy Spirit's prayer ministry will only come through identification with the cross of Jesus. As we reckon our old self dead in Christ through faith (Rom.

6:6,11,13), our new man is free to engage and be led by the Spirit of the Lord.

The deeper the realization we have of our true inabilities and emptiness before God, the more we will see our need to mortify the activity of the fleshly man. (Col. 3:5) Throughout our lives, the Lord is continually revealing to us areas where we trust in our own wisdom and strength rather than looking to Christ. Even our advancement in knowledge through years of studying and walking with Jesus becomes an area Satan uses to exalt us in pride. If we begin considering ourselves advanced, we open up to high-mindedness and self-exaltation, and thereby abort our access to the strength of the Holy Spirit. Identification with Jesus and his death on the cross reduces us to faith and love.

Reduced to Faith

As we identify with the cross of Christ, we are reduced to faith. As we take our position on Calvary's cross with Jesus, we fully acknowledge our inability. This identification compels us to look for strength and power outside of ourselves. This is the operating arena of faith and the realm governed by the Holy Spirit. Out of our strength and power, and by faith, into the strength and power of the Spirit. Let us think of this as the *look of faith*. We must look at Calvary, confess of our inability, and look to Jesus as our life, strength, and power. One of the major ministries of the Holy Spirit is to bring us to this position of death. Why? Because *out of this death* flows the life of the Spirit through us.

Reduced to Love

The Lord is also reducing us to love. (Greek, *agapē)* God's love involves an absolute surrender or sacrifice. We relinquish our rights when we walk in God's love. In the case of prayer, we surrender our *independent life* and selfish desires which are based in the old man. We willingly lay down the activity of our flesh, and by faith take up the activity of Jesus through our new creation in Christ. We discover the beauty of surrender. It is "no more I, but Christ in me." (Gal. 2:20) The Lord must give us the spiritual vision which is necessary to grasp our true inability. Lip service and spiritual sounding clichés will not produce the necessary insight we need. Neither will they reduce us to this position of love and surrender required to *pray in the Spirit.* Jesus said,

> *"I am the vine, ye are the branches: He that abideth in me, and I in him, the same bringeth forth much fruit: for without me ye can do nothing." (John 15:5)*

This abiding is an abiding in love. Not a worldly love, but the love of God (*agapē*) which calls us to lay down our life for others and for God. We will not appreciate this call of absolute sacrifice *until* we embrace the truth that apart from Jesus *we can do nothing.* (Jn. 15:5) It is easy for us to exalt the dynamics of faith in our prayer life, and that is good because apart from faith it is impossible to please God. (Heb. 11:6) But, let us realize that the dynamics of faith operate through and by the force of love. Paul said, *"Faith worketh by love."*

(Gal. 5:6) If we desire to go deeper into faith, we must pursue a deeper walk in the sacrificial love of God.

If we do not lay our fleshly deeds and self-strength down, our faith will not be able to lead us into true prayer or bring us into the power of the Holy Spirit. Why? Because it will not be biblical faith. We must see ourselves positionally crucified with Christ. (Rom. 6:6) Then, we must embrace this crucifixion as a *present reality* of our death and life. (Rom. 6:11) And finally, by faith, we must surrender to the work of the Holy Spirit to make this a living and conscious reality in our life. (Rom. 6:13)

The Lord desires to reduce us to love. Because God's love is a sacrificial love, when we surrender to it, we understand the call to sacrifice our desires for God's desires. Each year the Lord will bring us into a more insightful realization of this work of Calvary, and as a result, we begin to walk more in the realization of praying in the Spirit.

Praying in the Strength of the Holy Spirit

Based upon what we have developed throughout this book, and especially in this chapter, we now have the call from our Lord to pray in the *strength* of the Spirit. When we identify with the cross of Christ and apply its living work into our life, the wings of the Holy Spirit will sustain and carry us into and through our prayers. This is the place the Lord is pleading for us to enter. Prayer is a bold and refreshing discipline in the life of a believer—but only as we learn to perform it through God's strength.

We must refuse to abide in the shadow of man's prayer patterns or his information about prayer. These will only generate the work of the flesh. Instead, let us seek refuge in the presence of the Holy Spirit and allow him to take charge of our prayers. From this position comes not only the substance of our prayer, but also the strength and power of the Holy Spirit to offer it in faith. The Holy Spirit convicts us that we *need* to pray, *prompts us* what to pray, and then *enables us* to pray it in the Spirit.

Prayer:

Father, reduce us from our own strength and wisdom into Your love and faith. Teach us to embrace the death and life of Calvary's cross that we may be able to stand in the sufficient power of the Holy Spirit. Remove every hidden motive we may have when we pray, which seeks our glory and not Yours. Lead us, oh Lord, to life out of death and strength out of weakness. In Jesus name, Amen!

Chapter 12

Answering Our Questions

We began this book with three questions related to praying in the Spirit. What is it? Who can do it? How do we do it? Now we will answer them.

What is Praying in the Spirit?

Simply put, *praying in the Spirit* involves one of the most important spiritual disciplines relating to our prayer life. It is the practice of God's children to know the will of God *before* they offer prayers. When we know God's will, we are able to have confidence and assurance that the Lord will accomplish what we pray.

Discovering God's will is not always easy, especially when it relates to things which are not explicitly stated in the Scriptures. Even when things are clearly taught in the Bible, we must search to find God's will for *our* life. For example, we know that healing is included in the atonement. Jesus' death on Calvary provided the grounds for physical and spiritual healing. After all, the resurrection of the dead is the final or perfect physical healing which we all look for. However, we also see times when the Lord has a higher purpose in this life than physical healing—like revealing the power of His grace through our suffering. (2Cor. 12:8-10)

Most of us know Christians who have been healed of cancer, and we also know some who died from it. Healing is not a cut and dried benefit to take as an absolute for every situation on this side of eternity. Of course, we know God can, but the question is whether it is his will for our present circumstance. Those who give hurting souls a false hope with the "everybody will be healed if they have enough faith" doctrine, are ignorant of the Scriptures at best, and full of manipulation and deceit at worst.

Praying in the Spirit is work because it requires us to have a desperate pursuit for God, and it calls us to *wait patiently* before him in order to discern his will for our situation. The call to wait includes our willingness and desire to submit to the will of God. God calls us to *"be still and know I am God."* (Psa. 46:10) And it is the Holy Spirit who *reveals* the deep things of God to us. (1Cor. 2:9-10)

Praying in the Spirit is the practice of listening to the Lord *more than* we talk to Him. In other words, we stop the monologue version of prayer where we do all the talking, telling the Lord what we want. Instead, we begin prayer with quietness, waiting for Him to direct us about what and how to pray. (Rom. 8:26-27)

Praying in the Spirit is simply asking God, "Lord, what is your will in this situation?" Then, we wait for the conviction and impression of the Holy Spirit to make God's will known to us through his illumination. Afterwards, we evaluate it to make sure it does not contradict the Scriptures, and then we offer it to the Lord in prayer with faith and thankfulness.

Who Can do It?

Every true believer can pray *in the Spirit.* It is not a practice which requires any one gift. Neither is it a kind of prayer only available for a special class of Christians. Praying in the Spirit is the right and privilege of every child of God. *If we are born of the Spirit, we can pray in the Spirit!*

Other than being born-again, the only requirements for praying in the Spirit are a willingness to wait, discipline in hearing the Lord's voice, spiritual discernment, submission to the Lord's will, and faith. If the Lord can trust us, it is amazing what he will reveal to us about his will for our life. The call to pray in the Spirit will draw us into a deeper walk with Christ. We discover the freedom and closeness to walk as a disciple of Jesus Christ.

If you are one of God's children, you can pray in the Spirit. After all, Paul said every prayer is to be *in the Spirit.* We must refuse to let prayer become a meaningless exercise of futility by praying *our wants* instead of God's will. When we do, our prayer life will never be the same, and our intimacy with Christ will blossom.

HOW DO WE DO IT?

Praying in the Spirit is a call for us to get alone with the Lord and follow a couple of essential actions. *First,* we must get quiet to hear His voice. Our first order of business is to seek to know God's will. This means we begin by either voicing with our words, or with the words of our heart, questions to the Lord to show us His will for the situation we are facing.

Second, we listen for the guidance of the Holy Spirit. Many times, this requires sufficient time for our spirit to become quiet and free from distraction. We seek His guidance from a position of quietness and submission—not from passivity. This is where biblical meditation plays a key role.

Third, after we feel we have uncovered or discerned the Lord's will, we must evaluate it to make sure it passes the truth test. That test is to make sure the impression we feel does not contradict the authority or teaching of God's Word.[22]

Fourth, when we are convinced we have God's will, we pray it *in faith*. We cannot over emphasize this. The work of prayer is an exercise of faith. We must have faith (belief) that God wants to speak to us. We must make our request to know his will in faith. We must receive his guidance in

---

[22] For a detail discussion on how to evaluate impressions, see my book *"Trying the Spirits."*

prayer through faith. We must offer the prayer he shows us in faith, and then we must expect the answer through faith. Biblical faith can never be separated from the will of God. Any attempt to exercise faith toward God apart from agreeing with his sovereign will is nothing more than wishful thinking.

Fifth, after praying what we are convinced is God's will, we thank the Lord for the certainty of knowing that He hears us and will grant our petition. Because we have asked according to His will, we have confidence that the answer is granted and on the way! (1Jn. 5:14-15)

Sixth, through faith, we expectantly wait for the substance of the prayer to become a reality in life. It is already settled in our hearts, but we face a battle with the powers of darkness over standing firm in the promises of God. During this time, we find ourselves in the battle of faith. Satan will bring all types of doubt, discouragement, and attacks to dissuade us from standing in faith regarding what we believe to be the Lord's will.

Seventh, when the substance of the prayer becomes evident in the natural realm, we thank the Lord for his faithfulness toward us. This *is not* the first time we give thanks to him for the answer. When we offer the prayer in faith, and are waiting for the manifestation of the answered prayer, the posture of faith will continually thank the Lord for the answer which is *on the way*. Because we allowed God to *begin* the prayer, we have confidence that he will answer it.

A Final Question

What if we receive nothing when we ask the Lord to show us his will? What do we do and how can we pray in the Spirit in those times?

Assuming we have faithfully waited on the Lord for his guidance about what to pray, we proceed along an altered route. We search the Scriptures and discern all the *possibilities* of God's will which could be involved. For example, Paul requested to be healed of his affliction. He knew that the Lord is the healer, and had seen many miracles throughout his ministry. Paul continued to present a request for healing —three times. Though he did not have specific leadership concerning his affliction, he prayed what he felt was *most likely* to be God's will.

However, just because the Lord had not shown him the perfect will concerning his malady, Paul *remained open* for the Lord to change the direction of his request. After three requests for healing, the Lord spoke to Paul and gave him the understanding of his will. It involved Paul seeing and submitting to a deeper purpose through his affliction. Paul yielded and changed his prayer to match the heart, mind, and perfect will of God for his situation. If we are going to *pray in the Spirit*, we must do likewise.

The Lord uses these times of silence to compel us into a deeper study of the Word. As we search for his will in the

Scriptures, we may find several possibilities that relate to our situation. We should pray that which appears most likely to be his will. At the same time, we must *remain open* for the Holy Spirit to guide us into a more insightful understanding. There are many things the Lord is doing on many different levels, and the most essential thing for us is that we remain open to hear his voice and be willing to say, *"not my will, but thy will be done."*

Prayer:

Father, after we read and study your Word concerning prayer, convict us over our lack of prayer. Burn into our hearts that it is not information about prayer, but prayer itself that is our calling. We offer ourselves to you as vessels for Your work. Here we are Lord...here we are! In Jesus name, Amen!

Chapter 13

A Final Word

My prayer for those who have read this book is that each one will continue to search for spiritual truths concerning prayer, and that all of our prayers would be *"in the Spirit."* Our Lord has many treasures for His children if we will spend time with Him in prayer for sweet and holy communion. I encourage you to read books by some of the old saints who have written about prayer. There are many treasures awaiting you through some of them who have already finished their journey on earth.

We will always find that God is waiting for us to come to our private place of prayer. He desires to nurture and encourage us in the faith as we enjoy His presence. If we come by faith, His love will be our strength and our comfort. *Let us give ourselves to prayer.* For, as God's children, prayer is not only our duty, but it is our privilege. We truly understand this whenever prayer becomes the *delight* of our walk with Christ, and it will become a delight when we learn to *pray in the Spirit.*

There is no amount of reading about prayer which takes the place of actually praying. We must never substitute knowledge about prayer for the act of praying. There is much work to be performed by the church in our generation for revival and the planting of churches. Let us be committed to pray... to pray frequently...to pray in faith...and to pray *in the Spirit.* If it is true *"we have not because we ask not,"* then let us make sure we are asking. (Jas. 4:2)

Please pray for me as you enter the presence of our Lord, and I promise to pray for you. If we never get to pray together in this life, may we look for one another when the saints from all the ages gather around His Throne.

In the Crucified, yet Risen Lamb,

Terry

Author Profile

Terry Ivy is a husband, father, pastor, speaker, author and church planter. He surrendered to Christ in 1980 at the age of 18 and entered full time ministry in 1985. He is the author of many books dealing with the life of the believer and helping leaders understand some of the complex issues of ministry.

He is also the founder of *Project India*, a ministry which trains indigenous church planters to take the gospel to rural and unreached areas of India. From December of 2011 through May of 2024, he has overseen the planting of 412 churches in these areas with over 89,000 new converts from Islam and Hinduism. He, along with his wife Susanne, established an orphanage in India which cares for 16 children.

Terry's passion is to share God's Word to challenge and encourage leaders and believers, and to share God's love and truth to those who do not know Jesus as their Lord and Savior. Meeting, encouraging and spending time with other believers, especially leaders, is one of the great joys of his life. Terry has spent his life pouring over God's Word in order to understand the treasures the Lord has given us.

In 2008, he was diagnosed with cancer and experienced the horrors of chemotherapy and radiation. However, he will tell anyone that those times were 'painfully precious,' and brought the understanding of God's heart even closer in his life. He is working on a devotional book about affliction in the believer's life for those going through suffering.

Terry and Susanne were high school sweethearts and have been married since 1983. They have three grown and married boys: Joshua (1987) and his wife Erika, Joseph (1989) and his wife Julie, and Joel (1992) and his wife Katie. Terry and Susanne are the proud grandparents of six grandchildren, Jagger, Grace, Ledger, Eli, Revel, and Sparrow. Terry lives in Mississippi but is available for travel and speaking engagements.

For contact info or to order books visit: www.terryivy.com

Other Books by Terry Ivy

Purchase in Paperback or Kindle from Amazon

****

Trying the Spirits

Christian Discernment

Lessons from a Tax Collector

Studies in Matthew

Three Types of Division

Understanding the Good, the Bad, the Ugly

Restorative Church Discipline

Rescuing and Healing the Wounded

www.ingramcontent.com/pod-product-compliance
Ingram Content Group UK Ltd.
Pitfield, Milton Keynes, MK11 3LW, UK
UKHW040021200726
13854UKWH00001B/299